FOOD LOVERS

FISH AND SEAFOOD

FOOD LOVERS

FISH AND SEAFOOD

RECIPES SELECTED BY MARIKA KUCEROVA

Trans
Atlantic
Press

All recipes serve four people, unless otherwise indicated.

For best results when cooking the recipes in this book, buy fresh ingredients and follow the instructions carefully. Make sure that everything is properly cooked through before serving, particularly any meat and shellfish, and note that as a general rule vulnerable groups such as the very young, elderly people, pregnant women, convalescents and anyone suffering from an illness should avoid dishes that contain raw or lightly cooked eggs.

For all recipes, quantities are given in standard U.S. cups and imperial measures, followed by the metric equivalent. Follow one set or the other, but not a mixture of both because conversions may not be exact. Standard spoon and cup measurements are level and are based on the following:

1 tsp. = 5 ml, 1 tbsp. = 15 ml, 1 cup = 250 ml / 8 fl oz.

Note that Australian standard tablespoons are 20 ml, so Australian readers should use 3 tsp. in place of 1 tbsp. when measuring small quantities.

The electric oven temperatures in this book are given for conventional ovens with top and bottom heat. When using a fan oven, the temperature should be decreased by about 20–40ºF / 10–20ºC – check the oven manufacturer's instruction book for further guidance. The cooking times given should be used as an approximate guideline only.

CONTENTS

SALMON CURRY SOUP

Ingredients

½ small fresh pineapple

1 small apple

1 banana

1 onion

1 red chili

3 tbsp ghee or clarified butter

1 tbsp curry powder

1 tsp curcuma (turmeric)

4 tbsp coconut milk

475 ml / 2 cups chicken broth (stock)

225 ml / 1 cup milk

Salt and pepper

450 g / 1 lb asparagus spears

350 g / 12 oz salmon fillet

1 tsp lemon juice

Chopped fresh parsley, to garnish

Method

Prep and cook time: 40 min

1 Remove the skin from the pineapple and cut the flesh into small pieces. Peel the apple and cut into small pieces. Slice the banana.

2 Finely chop the onion. Slice the chili into rings, discarding the seeds, and set aside. Heat 1 tbsp of the ghee in a saucepan. Add the onion and fry until softened but not browned. Sprinkle the curry powder and curcuma (turmeric) over the onion and cook for 1 minute.

3 Add the fruit to the onion and heat quickly. Add the coconut milk, broth (stock) and milk and bring to the boil.

4 Remove from the heat and, using a hand-held blender, blend to form a purée. Season to taste with salt and pepper.

5 Cut the asparagus spears into small lengths and cook in a saucepan of boiling salted water for about 5 minutes, until tender but still firm to the bite. Drain and leave to dry.

6 Cut the salmon into bite-sized pieces, drizzle over the lemon juice and season with salt.

7 Heat the remaining 2 tbsp ghee or clarified butter in a non-stick skillet (frying pan). Add the salmon and quickly fry on both sides over a very high heat. Remove from the pan and keep warm. Quickly fry the asparagus in the same pan.

8 Serve the hot soup in small bowls, add the salmon and the asparagus and sprinkle the chili rings over the top. Garnish with parsley.

ASIAN FISH AND NOODLE SOUP

Ingredients

2 swordfish steaks, skinned

1 potato

8 scallions (spring onions)

2 garlic cloves

1 bird's eye chili

225 g / 8 oz snow peas (mange tout)

675 g / 1½ lb egg noodles

Salt and pepper

1.2 litres / 5 cups hot vegetable broth (stock)

2 tsp soy sauce

Lime wedges, to serve

Sprigs of fresh cilantro (coriander), to garnish

Method

Prep and cook time: 25 min

1 Cut the fish into bite-sized pieces. Finely slice the potato. Slice the scallions (spring onions). Crush the garlic. Very finely slice the chili, discarding the seeds. Cut the snow peas (mange tout) in half diagonally.

2 Plunge the noodles into boiling salted water, cook for 4 minutes, then drain.

3 Meanwhile, pour the broth (stock) into a large saucepan and bring to a simmer. Add the soy sauce, potato, scallions, garlic, chili and fish. Season with salt and pepper and simmer for 5 minutes.

4 Add the noodles and snow peas and warm through for 2–3 minutes.

5 Serve in bowls with lime wedges and garnish with cilantro (coriander).

CURRIED FISH SOUP WITH COCONUT

Ingredients

1 large onion

1 walnut sized piece fresh ginger

2 garlic cloves

2 tbsp Madras curry paste

1 tsp ground coriander

8 saffron threads

2 tbsp lemon juice

375 ml / 1²/₃ cups coconut milk

2 sticks lemon grass

450 g / 1 lb halibut fillet

Salt and pepper

4 scallions (spring onions), to garnish

Finely chopped chili (optional), to garnish

Method

Prep and cook time: 20 min

1 Roughly chop the onion. Peel and finely chop the ginger. Crush the garlic. Put the onions, ginger, garlic, curry paste, coriander, saffron and lemon juice in a food processor and blend together.

2 Add half the coconut milk and blend until combined.

3 Pour the remaining coconut milk into a wok or saucepan over a medium heat and add the spice mixture. Chop the lemon grass into 5 cm / 2 inch lengths and add to the pan. Stir and simmer for 5 minutes.

4 Meanwhile, cut the fish into bite-sized pieces. Add to the mixture and cook for a further 5 minutes, adding water, if necessary, to make the consistency of soup. Season to taste with salt and pepper.

5 Finely chop the scallions (spring onions). Serve the soup sprinkled with the chopped scallions and chili, if desired, to garnish.

HADDOCK CHOWDER

Ingredients

450 g / 1 lb haddock fillet, skinned

2 onions

3 celery stalks (sticks)

225 g / 8 oz new potatoes

40 g / 3 tbsp butter

125 g / 4 oz diced pancetta (optional)

1.2 liters / 5 cups milk

Salt and pepper

1 tbsp chopped fresh thyme, to garnish

Method

Prep and cook time: 40 min

1 Cut the fish into chunks. Slice the onions. Chop the celery. Cut 12 very thin slices of potato and cut the remaining potatoes into cubes.

2 Heat 2 tbsp butter in a large wide pan, add the onions and fry for 3 minutes. Add the pancetta pieces, if using, and cook for a further 5 minutes.

3 Heat the remaining butter in a clean pan, add the potato slices and fry gently until golden brown. Set aside.

4 Pour the milk into a large saucepan and heat to simmering point. Add the potatoes cubes and celery. Season with salt and pepper and cook gently for 10 minutes.

5 Carefully add the haddock to the pan and simmer for 5 minutes until the fish is just cooked. Serve in individual bowls garnished with the potato slices and thyme.

WHITEBAIT WITH CAPER DIP

Ingredients

Vegetable oil, for deep frying

900 g / 2 lb whitebait

4 tbsp all-purpose (plain) flour

¼ tsp cayenne pepper

Salt and pepper

Lemon wedges, to garnish

For the caper dip:

50 g / ⅓ cup baby gherkins

150 ml / ⅔ cup mayonnaise

Grated zest and juice 1 lemon

50 g / ⅓ cup capers

Method

Prep and cook time: 30 min

1 To make the caper dip, finely chop the gherkins. Put in a bowl, add the mayonnaise, lemon zest, juice of ½ the lemon and the capers and mix together. Add more lemon juice to taste. Turn into a serving bowl.

2 Half fill a deep fat fryer or large heavy-based saucepan with oil and heat to 170°C / 325°F.

3 Wash the whitebait and pat dry with paper towels (kitchen paper).

4 Put the flour in a large polythene (plastic) bag with the cayenne and plenty of salt and pepper.

5 Add the whitebait, seal the bag and toss together so that the fish is coated in the flour.

6 Deep fry a few handfuls of the whitebait at a time for 2–3 minutes, until crisp. Drain on paper towels and repeat with the remaining fish.

7 Season with salt and serve with the caper dip, garnished with lemon wedges.

FISH PIES

Ingredients

225 g / 8 oz salmon fillet

225 g / 8 oz pollock or cod fillet

1 onion

1 bay leaf

4 peppercorns

475 ml / 2 cups milk

7 tbsp white wine

Salt and pepper

For the topping:

900 g / 2 lb potatoes

7 tbsp milk

115 g / 1 stick butter

125 g / 4 oz grated Cheddar cheese

For the sauce:

40 g / 3 tbsp butter

3 tbsp all-purpose (plain) flour

3 tbsp whipping cream

Salt and pepper

1 bunch scallions (spring onions)

Method

Prep and cook time: 1 hr 30 min

1 Preheat the oven to 190°C (375°F / Gas Mark 5). Cut the salmon and pollock or cod fillet into bite-sized pieces, discarding any skin. Quarter the onion.

2 Put the fish into a large roasting pan. Add the onion, bay leaf, peppercorns, milk and wine. Season with salt and pepper.

3 Cover the pan with foil and cook in the oven for 25 minutes until the fish is tender and flakes easily.

4 Meanwhile, make the topping. Peel the potatoes, cut into large chunks and put in a large saucepan of salted water. Cover, bring to the boil and simmer for about 20 minutes until tender. Drain and return the potatoes to the pan.

5 Add the milk and butter to the potatoes and heat for 3 minutes. Remove from the heat and mash together until smooth. Stir in half the cheese.

6 Increase the oven temperature to 200°C (400°F / Gas Mark 6). Divide the fish between 4 ovenproof dishes. Strain the milk from the roasting pan into a jug.

7 To make the sauce, melt the butter in a pan. Add the flour, stir until smooth and cook for 1 minute. Gradually add the flavored milk from the jug, stirring all the time, until smooth. Bring to the boil, stirring, and cook until thickened. Stir in the cream and season to taste with salt and pepper.

8 Cut each scallion (spring onion) into 4 pieces. Add the scallions to the sauce and pour over the fish. Spoon the mashed potato into a piping bag fitted with a large star nozzle and pipe over the fish filling. Alternatively, spoon and spread over with a fork.

9 Put the dishes on to a baking sheet. Sprinkle over the remaining grated cheese and bake in the oven for 30 minutes until golden brown.

CATFISH WITH CRESS SAUCE

Ingredients

900 g / 2 lb potatoes

Salt and pepper

1 shallot

100g / 7 tbsp butter

125 ml / ½ cup dry white wine

7 tbsp whipping cream

2–3 tbsp cress

2 tbsp lemon juice

4 catfish or rockfish fillets, each weighing about 150 g / 5–6 oz

2–3 tbsp all-purpose (plain) flour

Lemon wedges, to garnish

Method

Prep and cook time: 40 min

1 Peel the potatoes, cut into large chunks and put in a saucepan of salted water. Cover, bring to the boil and simmer for about 15 minutes, until just tender.

2 Meanwhile, chop the shallot. Melt 50 g / 2 tbsp of the butter in a saucepan. Add the shallot and fry for about 1 minute until transparent.

3 Pour in the wine and cook over a medium heat until reduced by about a half. Stir in the cream and season to taste with salt and pepper. Add the cress.

4 Drizzle the lemon juice over the fish fillets. Sprinkle with salt and pepper and dredge with the flour. Shake off any excess flour.

5 Heat 3 tbsp butter in the pan and fry the fillets over medium heat for 2–3 minutes, on each side, until golden brown.

6 Drain the potatoes, return to the pan and heat briefly and allow some of the remaining cooking water to evaporate. Add the remaining butter and carefully coat the potatoes.

7 Serve the fish fillets and potatoes on warmed plates and drizzle the sauce over the top. Garnish with a lemon wedge.

HERB AND GARLIC SHRIMP SKEWERS

Ingredients

2 garlic cloves

12 large raw shrimp (tiger prawns)

Salt and pepper

Grated zest and juice of 2 limes

2 tbsp finely chopped fresh cilantro (coriander)

4 tbsp olive oil

Method

Prep and cook time: 15 min plus 2 hrs marinating

1 Crush the garlic. Put the shrimp (prawns) into a bowl, season with salt and pepper and add the garlic.

2 Add the lime zest and juice, cilantro (coriander) and olive oil and stir together. Cover and chill in the refrigerator for 2 hours to marinate.

3 Preheat the broiler (grill). Thread the shrimp on to 8 wooden skewers. Broil (grill) the shrimp for 5–10 minutes until they turn pink, turning occasionally.

COD FILLETS AU GRATIN

Ingredients

550 g / 1¼ lb floury potatoes

Salt and pepper

2 tomatoes

1 red onion

2 leeks

2 tbsp olive oil

3 tbsp breadcrumbs

3 tbsp freshly grated Parmesan cheese

2 tbsp thinly sliced basil leaves

70 g / 5 tbsp butter, plus extra
for greasing

¼ tsp grated nutmeg

5 tbsp milk

4 cod fillets, each weighing about
150 g / 5–6 oz each

2–3 tbsp lime juice

1 tbsp vegetable oil

Method

Prep and cook time: 1 hr

1 Peel the potatoes, cut into large chunks and put in a saucepan of salted water. Cover, bring to the boil and simmer for about 20 minutes, until tender.

2 Meanwhile, chop the tomatoes, discarding the seeds. Chop the onion and finely slice the leeks. Heat the olive oil in a skillet (frying pan), add the onion and fry until transparent. Add the tomatoes and cook for a further 5 minutes.

3 Remove the onions and tomatoes from the pan and put in a large bowl. Add the breadcrumbs, Parmesan cheese and basil leaves and mix together. Season with salt and pepper and set aside.

4 Heat 25 g / 2 tbsp of the butter in the pan, add the leeks and fry 5–10 minutes until softened.

5 Drain the potatoes, return to the pan and add the milk. Mash until smooth then season with salt, pepper and the nutmeg. Stir in the leeks.

6 Preheat the broiler (grill) to its highest setting. Lightly butter an ovenproof dish.

7 Season the cod fillets with the lime juice, salt and pepper. Heat the remaining butter and vegetable oil in the pan and gently fry the fillets for 2–3 minutes on each side.

8 Place the fish fillets in the prepared dish. Cover with the tomato mixture and broil (grill) for about 2 minutes. Serve on warmed plates with the mashed potatoes and leeks.

WARM SOLE AND SPINACH SALAD

Ingredients

4 tbsp all-purpose (plain) flour

4 fillets lemon sole

2 tbsp olive oil

For the mustard dressing:

4 tbsp olive oil

2 tbsp lemon juice

2 tsp wholegrain mustard

2 tbsp cold water

Salt and pepper

For the salad:

1 scallion (spring onion), chopped

2 eating apples, peeled and cored

150 g / 5 cups baby spinach leaves

Method

Prep and cook time: 30 min

1 To make the dressing, put the olive oil, lemon juice, mustard, water, salt and pepper in a jar with a lid. Cover and shake to mix together. Set aside.

2 To prepare the salad, chop the scallion (spring onion). Peel, core and roughly chop the apples. Arrange the spinach leaves on a serving plate.

3 Spread the flour on to a large plate and season with salt and pepper. Coat the fish fillets in the seasoned flour.

4 Heat the olive oil in a large skillet (frying pan). Add the fish fillets and fry for 4–5 minutes on each side until lightly browned.

5 Serve the sole on top of the spinach and sprinkle over the apples and scallion. Shake the mustard dressing and drizzle over to serve.

SALMON AND LEEK *SKEWERS*

Ingredients

675 g / 1½ lb salmon fillet

3 red bell peppers

2 leeks

1 garlic clove

Salt and pepper

4 tbsp vegetable oil

2 tbsp rosemary leaves

½ tsp grated zest lemon

Method

Prep and cook time: 20 min

1 Preheat the broiler (grill). Cut the salmon into cubes. Chop the red peppers into bite-sized pieces, discarding the core and seeds. Slice the leeks into 3 cm / 1 inch pieces.

2 Thread salmon, pepper and leek chunks alternately on to wooden skewers.

3 Using the back of a knife, crush the garlic with a little salt. Put in a bowl, add the oil, rosemary and lemon zest and stir together.

4 Brush the oil over the kebabs and broil (grill) for 4–6 minutes, turning several times and basting occasionally with the oil. Season with salt and pepper before serving.

FILLETS WITH A POTATO CRUST

Ingredients

4 large potatoes

4 chunky white fish fillets, such as turbot, flounder, halibut

Salt and pepper

115 g / 1 stick butter, plus extra to grease

16 cherry tomatoes

2 garlic cloves

450 g / 1 lb baby spinach leaves

Finely grated zest and juice 1 lemon

200 g / 1 cup crème fraîche

2 tbsp dry vermouth

Method

Prep and cook time: 40 min

1 Preheat the oven to 200°C (400°F / Gas Mark 6). Butter a roasting pan.

2 Peel the potatoes, cut into large chunks and put in a saucepan of water. Cover, bring to the boil and simmer for about 10 minutes. Drain and coarsely grate the potatoes. Put in a bowl and season with salt and pepper.

3 Lay the fish in the prepared pan, season with salt and pepper and cover each piece with the grated potato.

4 Melt the butter and drizzle a quarter over each potato topped fish fillet.

5 Bake in the oven for 15 minutes. Meanwhile, cut the tomatoes into quarters. Crush the garlic.

6 Add the tomatoes, garlic, spinach leaves, lemon zest and juice to the pan and return to the oven for 10 minutes until the spinach has wilted and the tomatoes are beginning to char.

7 Put the crème fraîche and vermouth into a small saucepan and heat gently.

8 To serve, place the spinach and tomatoes on to warmed serving plates, top with the fish and serve with the vermouth crème fraîche.

FRIED TROUT WITH ROSTI

Ingredients

4 trout fillets, with skin on

1 tbsp lemon juice

Salt and pepper

1 tbsp vegetable oil

15 g / 1 tbsp butter

For the rosti:

900 g / 2 lb floury potatoes

1 onion

200 g / 1¼ cups frozen peas, thawed

Grated nutmeg

Salt and pepper

2 tbsp all-purpose (plain) flour

1 egg

150 ml / ⅔ cup vegetable oil

25 g / 2 tbsp butter

Method

Prep and cook time: 45 min

1 Preheat the oven to its lowest setting. To make the Rosti, finely grate the potatoes. Put on a tea towel and squeeze to remove excess water. Turn into a bowl.

2 Finely chop the onion. Add to the potato with the peas and mix together. Season with nutmeg, salt and pepper. Add the flour and egg and knead together. Form the mixture into flat rounds.

3 Heat the oil and butter in a skillet (frying pan), add the rosti, one at a time, and fry until golden brown, turning once. Transfer to a plate and put in the oven to keep warm.

4 Cut the fish into 5 cm / 2 inch long pieces. Drizzle over the lemon juice and season with salt and pepper.

5 Heat the oil and butter in a skillet, add the fish pieces, skin side down, and fry each piece for about 2 minutes. Turn the pieces over and cook for 1 more minute. Remove the pan from the heat.

6 Place the rosti on warmed serving plates and place the fish on top.

PLAICE ROLLS
WITH ORANGE BUTTER

Ingredients

4 sprigs thyme

4 garlic cloves

Salt and pepper

3 tbsp lemon juice

8 plaice or sole fillets, each weighing about 90 g / 3 oz

1 tsp cayenne pepper

¼ tsp grated nutmeg

¼ tsp ground cloves

2 oranges

75 g / 5 tbsp butter, plus extra for greasing

1 tsp sugar

2 tbsp orange liqueur

1 tbsp orange marmalade

Method

Prep and cook time: 30 min plus 20 min marinating

1 Preheat the oven to 220°C (425°F / Gas Mark 7). Lightly butter an ovenproof dish.

2 Remove the leaves from the thyme sprigs and chop finely. Crush the garlic with a little salt. Put the garlic and chopped thyme in a bowl. Add the lemon juice, mix together and leave to marinate for 20 minutes.

3 Sprinkle the fish fillets with the pepper, cayenne pepper, nutmeg and cloves. Divide the thyme mixture evenly over the fillets.

4 Roll up the fillets and secure with a wooden skewer or toothpick (cocktail stick). Place the fillets, side by side, in the prepared dish.

5 Squeeze the juice from 1 orange. Pour the juice evenly over the rolled fillets. Cover with foil and cook in the oven for about 15 minutes.

6 Remove the zest and squeeze the juice from the remaining orange. Melt the butter in a saucepan. Add the orange zest, juice and sugar and cook until the mixture caramelizes slightly. Add the orange liqueur, marmalade and season with salt and pepper.

7 To serve, place the rolled fillets on warmed serving plates and drizzle the sauce over the fillets. Serve immediately.

SEAFOOD PAELLA

Ingredients

450 g / 1 lb fresh mussels in shells

350 g / 12 oz prepared squid

1 onion

2 garlic cloves

1 red bell pepper

3 tomatoes

160 ml / 10 tbsp olive oil

1 liter / 4 cups vegetable broth (stock)

8 saffron threads

400 g / 2 cups short grain rice

1 handful frozen peas

300 g / 10 oz peeled shrimp (prawns)

Salt and pepper

2 tbsp chopped fresh parsley

Method

Prep and cook time: 1 hr

1 Preheat the oven to 200°C (400°F / Gas Mark 6). Clean the mussels by scrubbing the shells and pulling out any beards that are attached to them.

2 Roughly chop the squid. Chop the onion and garlic. Chop the red pepper, discarding the core and seeds. Cut the tomatoes in half.

3 Heat 5 tbsp of the olive oil in a large, deep saucepan. Add the onion and fry for about 5 minutes until softened. Add the garlic. Pour in half of the broth (stock) and bring to the boil. Add the mussels and simmer, uncovered, for 10 minutes.

4 Using a slotted spoon, transfer the mussels to a bowl, discarding any that have not opened. Set aside. Put a few spoonfuls of the hot broth in a small bowl. Add the saffron and allow to infuse.

5 Heat the remaining oil in a large paella pan. Add the rice and fry briefly, stirring continuously. Pour in the saffron broth, the onion/broth mixture and the remaining broth. Bring to the boil, stir and simmer for about 15 minutes.

6 Add the red pepper, tomatoes, peas, shrimp (prawns) and squid to the rice.

7 Cover the paella pan with foil and cook in the oven for about 20 minutes. Stir in the mussels 5 minutes before the end of the cooking time, and season with salt and pepper. Sprinkle over the parsley and serve.

MACKEREL WITH DIJON MUSTARD

Ingredients

Butter, for greasing

8 mackerel fillets

2 tbsp Dijon mustard

2 tsp chopped fresh oregano

1 tbsp chopped fresh cilantro
(coriander)

1 lemon

2 leeks

4 tbsp olive oil

Method

Prep and cook time: 25 min

1 Preheat the oven to 190°C (375°F / Gas Mark 5).
Grease a roasting pan.

2 Make 4 slashes through the skin side of each
mackerel fillet. Lay 4 fillets, skin side down, into the
roasting pan.

3 Spread the mustard over the flesh of the fillets in
the pan and sprinkle a little oregano and cilantro
(coriander) over each one. Cut the lemon in half and
squeeze the lemon juice over the fillets.

4 Finely chop the leeks and divide them between
the fillets. Drizzle over the olive oil and lay the
remaining fillets on top.

5 Bake in the oven for 15 minutes until the fish and
leeks are tender.

SWEET POTATO AND SHRIMP CAKES

Ingredients

225 g / 8 oz sweet potato

Salt and pepper

200 g / 7 oz canned chick peas, drained

1 small onion

1 garlic clove

450 g / 1 lb peeled cooked shrimp (prawns)

2 tbsp chopped fresh cilantro (coriander)

2 tbsp olive oil

Few sprigs of mint, to garnish

Lime wedges, to serve

For the raita:

10 cm / 4 inch piece cucumber

200 g / scant cup Greek yogurt

2 tbsp chopped fresh mint

For the dip:

2 tbsp sweet chili sauce

1 tsp dark soy sauce

Method

Prep and cook time: 40 min

1 Put the unpeeled sweet potato in a saucepan of salted water, bring to the boil and cook for 10 minutes. Let cool, peel and grate coarsely.

2 Put the chick peas in a food processor and blend until smooth or mash with a fork. Put in a bowl. Finely chop the onion and crush the garlic. Add to the bowl with the shrimp (prawns), sweet potato and cilantro (coriander) and mix together. Season with salt and pepper.

3 To make the raita, finely chop the cucumber and put in a bowl. Add the yogurt and mint and mix together. Put in a serving bowl.

4 To make the dip, stir the sweet chili sauce and soy sauce together and put in a serving bowl.

5 Form the potato and shrimp mixture into patties. Heat the oil in a skillet (frying pan), add the potato cakes and fry over a low heat for 2–3 minutes on each side until browned.

6 To serve, garnish with mint springs and lime wedges and serve with the dip and raita for dipping.

GRIDDLED SQUID BRUSCHETTA

Ingredients

1 garlic clove

1 red chili

450 g / 1 lb prepared squid

8 cherry tomatoes

2 tbsp olive oil

1 tbsp fresh rosemary sprigs, plus extra to garnish

Juice of ½ a lemon

1 ciabatta loaf

4 tbsp garlic mayonnaise

4 little gem lettuce leaves

Salt and pepper

Method

Prep and cook time: 30 min

1 Crush the garlic. Finely slice the chili, discarding the seeds. Slice the tomatoes. Cut the squid into 2 cm / 1 inch pieces.

2 Put the squid in a bowl, add the olive oil, garlic, chili, rosemary springs and lemon juice and mix together. Thread 2 squid pieces on to small wooden skewers.

3 Preheat the broiler (grill) and heat a ridged skillet (frying pan) or griddle pan. Cut the ciabatta bread in half horizontally and then vertically to make 4 pieces. Toast until light golden brown.

4 Spread each piece of toast with 1 tbsp of mayonnaise. Add a lettuce leaf and some sliced tomatoes to each.

5 Season the squid with salt and pepper, add to the hot skillet and cook for 1–2 minutes, turning once, until lightly charred.

6 Serve squid on top of the bruschetta garnished with a few rosemary sprigs.

SEA BASS AND VEGETABLES

Ingredients

1 onion

450 g / 1 lb potatoes

1 tbsp olive oil

1 red bell pepper

1 zucchini (courgette)

2 tbsp tomato paste

400 g / 14 oz canned chopped tomatoes

325 ml / 1^1/3 cups hot vegetable broth (stock)

Salt and pepper

8 sea bass or gray mullet fillets

1 tbsp olive oil

Juice of 1 lime

2 tbsp chopped chives, to garnish

Method

Prep and cook time: 40 min

1 Finely chop the onion. Peel and chop the potatoes. Cut the red pepper into dice, discarding the seeds. Dice the zucchini (courgette). Heat the oil in a large saucepan, add the onion and fry for about 5 minutes, until translucent.

2 Add the potatoes and cook for 2–3 minutes. Stir in the tomato paste, canned tomatoes and hot vegetable broth (stock). Season with salt and pepper and simmer for 15 minutes.

3 Add the red pepper and zucchini and simmer for 5 minutes.

4 Season the flesh side of the fish with salt and pepper. Heat the oil in a large heavy based skillet (frying pan) until hot, add the fish, skin-side down. When the skin of the fish is brown and crisp, turn the fish over and finish cooking for 2–3 minutes. Add a squeeze of lime juice.

5 Serve the fish on top of the vegetable stew and garnish with chopped chives.

GRILLED BASS
WITH CHILI AND BELL PEPPERS

Ingredients

1 walnut sized piece of fresh ginger

3 garlic cloves

2 red chilies

1 red bell pepper

1 yellow bell pepper

6 scallions (spring onions)

4 sea bass, cleaned, scaled and heads removed

Salt and pepper

3 tbsp sunflower oil

1 tbsp light soy sauce

Lemon wedges, to garnish

Method
Prep and cook time: 30 min

1 Peel and cut the ginger into matchsticks. Crush the garlic. Finely slice the chilies, red and yellow peppers, discarding the core and seeds. Cut the scallions (spring onions) into thin strips.

2 Using a sharp knife, slash the fish skin 2–3 times and season with salt and pepper.

3 Heat 1 tbsp oil in a heavy-based skillet (frying pan). Add the fish and fry for 5 minutes or until the skin is very crisp and golden. Turn over, cook for a further 5 minutes, or until the fish is cooked through.

4 Heat the remaining oil in another pan, add the ginger, garlic, chilies and peppers and fry for 2–3 minutes until softened. Remove from the heat and toss in the scallions.

5 Splash the fish with a little soy sauce and serve topped with the pepper mixture, garnished with lemon wedges.

BAKED FISH WITH LEEKS

Ingredients

2 tbsp olive oil, plus extra for greasing

6 scallions (spring onions)

4 leeks

Salt and pepper

4 fish fillets, such as halibut, pollock, salmon

600 ml / 2½ cups white wine

1 lemon

4 saffron threads

Method

Prep and cook time: 40 min

1 Preheat the oven to 190°C (375°F / Gas Mark 5). Grease a large roasting pan.

2 Finely chop the scallions (spring onions) and set aside. Slice the leeks. Blanch in boiling water for 5 minutes and then drain well.

3 Put the leeks into the prepared roasting pan. Season with salt and pepper and drizzle over 1 tbsp olive oil.

4 Top with the fish fillets and season with salt and pepper. Sprinkle over the scallions.

5 Pour the wine around the fish and squeeze over the lemon juice. Scatter with the saffron threads.

6 Cover with foil and bake in the oven for 25 minutes until the fish and leeks are tender.

SPICY SHRIMP SALAD

Ingredients

1 red onion

450 g / 1 lb cherry tomatoes

2 avocados

1 red chili

1 garlic clove

Salt and pepper

8 tbsp olive oil

4 tbsp lime juice

2 tbsp white wine vinegar

450 g / 1 lb cooked peeled shrimp (prawns)

4 tbsp chopped fresh cilantro (coriander) leaves

Method

Prep and cook time: 20 min

1 Slice the onion. Cut the tomatoes in half. Cut the avocados into quarters and slice the flesh. Finely chop the chili, discarding the seeds. Crush the garlic.

2 Put all the prepared vegetables into a large bowl. Season with salt and pepper.

3 Pour in the olive oil, lime juice and wine vinegar. Stir in the shrimp (prawns) and cilantro (coriander) leaves and toss together before serving.

SOLE AND SPINACH ROLLS

Ingredients

450 g / 1 lb spinach

40 g / ¼ cup mascarpone

1 tsp lemon zest

Grated nutmeg

Salt and pepper

1 egg yolk

8 sole fillets

1 shallot

40 g / 3 tbsp butter

2 tsp dry vermouth

150 ml / ⅔ cups fish broth (stock)

75 ml / ⅓ cup sparkling wine

75 ml / ⅓ cup whipping cream

Method
Prep and cook time: 45 min

1 Wash the spinach and put in a large saucepan with only the water clinging to its leaves and cook until wilted. Turn into a sieve and drain, squeezing out any excess water.

2 Chop a third of the spinach and put in a food processor. Add the mascarpone and blend to form a purée. Add the lemon zest and nutmeg and season with salt and pepper. Add the egg yolk and mix well together.

3 Spread the spinach mixture over each sole fillet. Roll up and secure with a toothpick (cocktail stick).

4 Finely chop the shallot. Heat 15 g / 1 tbsp of the butter in a saucepan, add the shallot and fry until softened. Add the vermouth and cook until reduced slightly. Add the fish broth (stock) and two-thirds of the sparkling wine and simmer gently for 2–3 minutes.

5 Place the sole rolls into the broth (stock), cover and poach for 4–5 minutes. Remove the fish rolls and keep warm.

6 Strain the cooking liquid through a sieve into a jug. Add half the cream and return to the saucepan. Bring to the boil and cook until reduced by a third. Add the remaining cream and sparkling wine. Season to taste with salt and pepper.

7 Pour about a third of the sauce into a separate pan, add the remaining spinach and warm through.

8 Add the remaining butter to the remaining sauce and, using a hand-held blender, blend until frothy. Serve the sole rolls on the spinach and drizzle over the foamy sauce.

STUFFED SQUID WITH TOMATO SAUCE

Ingredients

2 slices white bread

7 tbsp milk

200 ml / ¾ cup fish broth (stock)

10 large raw peeled shrimp (prawns)

1 onion

3 garlic cloves

2 large fresh red chilies

2 tbsp olive oil

3 tbsp chopped fresh basil plus some to garnish

1 egg yolk

Salt and pepper

8 fresh prepared squid bodies

7 tbsp white wine

Two 400-g / 14-oz cans chopped tomatoes

Method

Prep and cook time: 40 min

1 Remove the crusts from the bread and tear into pieces. Put in a bowl, add the milk and let soak for 5 minutes. Squeeze to remove any excess milk.

2 Pour the broth (stock) into a medium saucepan and bring to a simmer. Add the shrimp (prawns) and simmer until they turn pink. Remove the cooked shrimp from the pan, retaining the fish broth.

3 Chop the shrimp. Finely chop the onion and crush the garlic. Finely chop the chilies, discarding the seeds. Heat 1 tbsp of the olive oil in a large saucepan over a low heat. Add the onion, one-third of the garlic and half of the chilies and cook for 5 minutes until softened but not browned.

4 Add the basil, the chopped shrimp, bread and egg yolk. Season with salt and pepper. Cook for about 3 minutes, stirring all the time to prevent the mixture from sticking, until the mixture is fairly dry.

5 Stuff the mixture into each squid body so that it is three-quarters full and carefully secure each with a toothpick (cocktail stick).

6 Heat 1 tbsp of olive oil in a large skillet (frying pan) and add the squid. Cook for about 10 minutes until lightly browned on both sides, turning frequently using the cocktail sticks. Remove from the pan and keep warm.

7 Add the remaining chili and the 2 garlic cloves to the pan and cook for a further 1 minute. Add the white wine and simmer for about 5 minutes.

8 Add the reserved fish broth and the tomatoes to the pan and simmer until the sauce has thickened. Season to taste with salt and pepper and return the squid to the pan to heat through. Serve garnished with chopped basil.

COD WITH MEDITERRANEAN VEGETABLES

Ingredients

5 tbsp olive oil, plus extra for greasing

6 scallions (spring onions)

2 garlic cloves

2 eggplants (aubergines)

3 zucchini (courgettes)

2 tbsp fresh thyme leaves

Salt and pepper

4 cod fillets, total weight about 450 g / 1 lb

2 eggs

225 ml / 1 cup milk

150 ml / ²/₃ cups plain yogurt

Grated nutmeg

50 g / ½ cup grated Parmesan cheese

Method

Prep and cook time: 1 hr 20 min

1 Preheat the oven to 190°C (375°F / Gas Mark 5). Grease a large ovenproof dish. Thinly slice the scallions (spring onions). Chop the garlic. Cut the eggplants (aubergines) width ways and the zucchini (courgettes) lengthways, into 5 mm / ¼ inch slices.

2 Heat 2 tbsp of the oil in a skillet (frying pan), add the scallions and garlic and fry for 2–3 minutes. Stir in the thyme and remove from the heat.

3 Heat a little of the remaining oil in a ridged skillet or griddle. Add the eggplants and zucchini slices in batches and fry for 1–2 minutes, each side, until golden brown. Add more oil between batches. Season with salt and pepper and set aside.

4 Fill the prepared dish with alternating layers of the fish, vegetables and scallion mixture.

5 Put the eggs, milk and yogurt in a jug and mix together. Season well with salt, pepper and nutmeg and pour over the vegetables and fish. Sprinkle over the Parmesan cheese.

6 Bake in the oven for 35–40 minutes until the top is golden brown.

INDONESIAN NOODLES WITH PRAWNS

Ingredients

6 scallions (spring onions)

2 onions

3 garlic cloves

175 g / 6 oz pak choi

2 red chilies

500 g / 1 lb 2 oz boneless chicken breasts, skinned or monkfish

350 g / 12 oz thin egg noodles

8 tbsp vegetable oil

1 tbsp finely chopped fresh ginger

225 g / 8 oz raw shrimp (prawns)

1 tsp sugar

2 tbsp light soy sauce

3 tbsp vegetable broth (stock)

Salt and pepper

Cilantro (coriander) leaves, to garnish

Method

Prep and cook time: 40 min

1 Chop the scallions (spring onions). Finely chop the onions. Crush the garlic. Cut the pak choi into quarters. Finely slice the chilies, discarding the seeds. Cut the chicken breasts or monkfish into 1.5 cm / ½ inch slices.

2 Cook the noodles in plenty of boiling, salted water according to the packet instructions and drain well.

3 Heat the oil in a wok or large skillet (frying pan), add the chicken or monkfish and stir-fry for 2–3 minutes until golden brown.

4 Add the scallions, onions and garlic and fry for 3 minutes. Add the pak choi, chili, ginger and the shrimp (prawns) and fry for a further 2 minutes. Add the sugar, soy sauce and stock and season with salt and pepper. Mix in the noodles and heat, stirring, until warm. Serve immediately.

CATFISH WITH HORSERADISH

Ingredients

100 ml / 7 tbsp white wine

Salt and pepper

4–6 sprigs fresh tarragon

50 g / 2 oz fresh horseradish root

200 ml / generous 2/3 cup vegetable broth (stock)

675 g / 1½ lb potatoes

4 catfish or rockfish fillets, total weight about 675 g / 1½ lb

2 carrots

90 g / 3 oz celery root (celeriac)

1 leek

Method

Prep and cook time: 40 min

1 Put the wine and broth (stock) in a large saucepan and bring to the boil. Season with salt and add half of the tarragon.

2 Peel and halve the horseradish. Put half into the wine and broth. Grate the other half and set aside.

3 Peel and cut the potatoes into cubes. Add the potatoes to the poaching liquid and cook for 5 minutes. Meanwhile, very thinly slice the carrots and celery root (celeriac). Slice the leek into very thin strips.

4 Season the fish fillets with salt and pepper. Add the fish, carrots, celery root and leek to the pan, cover and poach very gently for about 12 minutes, until the fish is tender. Remove the horseradish from the poaching liquid.

5 Serve the fish with the potatoes and vegetables in deep serving bowls. Sprinkle with the grated horseradish. Pour all little poaching liquid over the top and garnish with the remaining tarragon.

FISH CAKES WITH HOLLANDAISE SAUCE

Ingredients

450 g / 1 lb floury potatoes

3 tbsp milk

900 g / 2 lb pollock or cod fillet, skinned

Salt and pepper

1 tsp peppercorns

1 tbsp capers

Juice of 1 small lemon

2 tbsp chopped fresh dill

2 tbsp mayonnaise

3 tbsp all-purpose (plain) flour

Sunflower oil, for shallow frying

Sprigs of fresh dill, to garnish

For the Hollandaise sauce:

6oz / 1½ sticks butter

2 large egg yolks

1 tbsp white wine vinegar

1 tbsp lemon juice

Method

Prep and cook time: 45 min plus 30 min chilling time

1 Peel the potatoes, cut into large chunks and put in a saucepan of salted water. Cover, bring to the boil and simmer for about 20 minutes, until tender. Drain, return to the pan and add the milk. Mash until smooth. Let cool.

2 Meanwhile, put the fish into a wide saucepan, cover with cold, salted water and add the peppercorns. Bring to the boil and simmer for 5–7 minutes, or until the fish is opaque and flakes easily. Using a slotted spoon, lift the fish from the liquid and put into a bowl.

3 Roughly chop the capers. Add the capers, lemon juice, dill, mayonnaise and mashed potato to the fish. Season with salt and pepper and mix well together.

4 Dust a work surface with the flour and form the mixture into 8 fish cakes. Chill in the refrigerator for 30 minutes.

5 To make the Hollandaise sauce, melt the butter in a small saucepan over a medium heat, making sure it does not burn. Turn off the heat and allow the milky residue to settle to the bottom of the pan.

6 Put the egg yolks in a food processor, add the vinegar and lemon juice and blend for 15 seconds to thoroughly combine.

7 With the motor running, slowly drip the melted butter through the feeder tube, leaving the milky residue behind. Season with salt. To keep warm, put into a bowl standing in a saucepan of boiled water.

8 Heat the oil in a large skillet (frying pan), add the fish cakes and fry for 2–3 minutes on each side, turning once, until golden brown. Serve the fish cakes with the warm Hollandaise Sauce and garnish with fresh dill.

SHRIMP AND ASPARAGUS SALAD

Ingredients

300 g / 10 oz pasta bows

Salt

225 g / 8 oz asparagus

225 g / 8 oz snow peas (mange tout)

7 tbsp plain yogurt

3 tbsp mayonnaise

2 tbsp lemon juice

450 g / 1 lb cooked shrimp (prawns)

2 ripe avocados

1 tbsp chopped fresh dill, to garnish

Method

Prep and cook time: 30 min

1 Cook the pasta bows in a large pan of boiling, salted water according to the packet instructions or until tender but still firm to the bite. Drain, rinse under cold water, and put into a large bowl.

2 Cut the asparagus into 5 cm / 2 inch lengths. Blanch the asparagus and snow peas (mange tout) in boiling salted water for 2 minutes and then drain, plunge into cold water and drain again. Add to the pasta.

3 Put the yogurt, mayonnaise and lemon juice in a bowl and mix together. Stir into the pasta and vegetables. Season generously with salt and pepper. Add the shrimp (prawns).

4 Cut the avocados into quarters and peel away the skin. Remove the stone and slice the flesh. Gently stir into the pasta salad. Spoon into serving bowls and garnish with dill to serve.

TUNA WITH RICE NOODLE SALAD

Ingredients

175 g / 6 oz thin rice noodles

2 tsp sesame oil

2 tbsp soy sauce

1 tbsp chili sauce

1 tsp lime zest

4 tbsp lime juice

1 tbsp runny honey

5 tbsp olive oil

Salt and pepper

3 tbsp sesame seeds

1 red bell pepper

6 scallions (spring onions)

4 tuna steaks, each weighing about 175 g / 6 oz

4 tbsp vegetable oil

1 tsp coarsely ground mixed colored peppercorns

Method

Prep and cook time: 30 min plus 30 min soaking

1 Put the rice noodles in a bowl of warm water and let soak for 30 minutes to soften. Drain well, put in a bowl and stir in a little of the sesame oil.

2 To make the dressing, put the soy sauce, chili sauce, lime zest and juice, honey, remaining sesame oil and 3 tbsp of the olive oil in a large bowl and mix together. Season with salt.

3 Toast the sesame seeds in a dry non-stick skillet (frying pan). Remove from the pan and let cool.

4 Thinly slice the red peppers, discarding the core and seeds. Thinly slice the scallions (spring onions).

5 Heat the remaining olive oil in the pan, add the red peppers and fry for 3–4 minutes. Add the scallions and fry for a further 2 minutes. Season with salt. Add the hot vegetables to the dressing. Add the toasted sesame seeds and mix together.

6 Season the tuna steaks with salt and pepper. Heat the vegetable oil in the pan and fry the steaks on each side for 2–3 minutes.

7 Serve the tuna topped with the noodles and vegetables and sprinkle with coarsely ground pepper.

FRIED SCALLOPS WITH SALSA VERDE

Ingredients

For the salsa verde:

4 anchovy fillets

1 garlic clove

25 g / 1 cup chopped fresh parsley

25 g / 1 cup chopped fresh basil

25 g / 1 cup chopped fresh mint

2 tbsp capers

2 tbsp lemon juice

8 tbsp olive oil

Salt and pepper

25 g / 2 tbsp butter

12 shelled scallops

Method

Prep and cook time: 15 min

1 Finely chop the anchovies. Crush the garlic. Put the anchovies, garlic, parsley, basil, mint, capers and lemon juice in a food processor. Whilst the motor is running, gradually pour in the olive oil. Season to taste with salt and pepper.

2 Season the scallops with salt and pepper. Heat the butter in a skillet (frying pan), add the scallops and fry for just 2 minutes each side.

3 Serve the scallops with the salsa verde.

COD WITH TOMATO AND OLIVE CRUST

Ingredients

2 tbsp olive oil, plus extra for greasing

4 cod fillets

100 ml / 7 tbsp dry white wine

1 onion

2 garlic cloves

150 g / ⅓ cup pitted (stoned) black olives

12 pieces sun-blushed tomatoes, drained from oil

1 tbsp chopped fresh parsley

Method

Prep and cook time: 35 min

1 Preheat the oven to 180°C (350°F / Gas Mark 4). Grease an ovenproof dish.

2 Put the fish fillets into the dish and pour in the wine.

3 Chop the onion, garlic cloves and olives. Put in a bowl, add the sun-blushed tomatoes, parsley and olive oil and mix together.

4 Spread the tomato and olive mixture on top of the fish fillets.

5 Bake in the oven for 20 minutes until the fish flakes easily. If wished, serve with green (French) beans and roasted cherry tomatoes.

SEAFOOD SPAGHETTI

Ingredients

115 g / 4 oz string (runner) beans

Salt and pepper

450 g / 1 lb spaghetti

1 small onion

4 garlic cloves

2 tbsp olive oil

675 g / 1½ lbs mixed prepared seafood, thawed if frozen

125 ml / ½ cup vegetable broth (stock)

150 g / ⅔ cup crème fraîche

2–3 tbsp lemon juice

50 g / ½ cup grated Parmesan cheese

Basil leaves, to garnish

Method

Prep and cook time: 30 min

1 Cook the beans in a saucepan of boiling salted water for about 10 minutes until tender but still firm to the bite. Rinse under cold water and drain well.

2 Meanwhile, cook the spaghetti according to the instructions on the packet.

3 Chop the onion and garlic cloves. Heat the oil in a large saucepan, add the onion and garlic and fry for 2–3 minutes. Add the seafood and fry for a further 2–3 minutes.

4 Pour in the vegetable broth (stock) and bring to a boil. Stir in the crème fraîche. Reduce the heat and season with the lemon juice, salt and pepper. Stir in the beans and reheat them.

5 Drain the spaghetti and mix with the seafood sauce. Serve on warmed plates sprinkled with the Parmesan cheese. Garnish with the basil leaves.

KEDGEREE

Ingredients

2 eggs

450 g / 1 lb un-dyed smoked haddock fillets

2 bay leaves

200 g / 1 cup long grain rice

1 walnut sized piece fresh ginger

1 bunch scallions (spring onions)

1 garlic clove

115g / 1 stick butter

2 tbsp curry powder

Juice of 1 lemon, plus 4 lemon halves, to garnish

Method

Prep and cook time: 40 min

1 Put the eggs into a pan of boiling water and cook for 10 minutes. Rinse under cold running water to cool completely and then remove the shell.

2 Put the haddock and bay leaves in a shallow pan with enough water to cover. Bring to the boil, cover and simmer for about 5 minutes, until tender. Remove the pan from the heat and leave to cool. When cool, remove the skin and flake the flesh into chunks. Set aside.

3 Cook the rice according to the packet instructions.

4 Meanwhile, peel and grate the ginger. Finely chop the scallions (spring onions). Crush the garlic. Melt the butter in a pan over a low heat, add the ginger, scallions and garlic and cook for about 5 minutes until softened.

5 Add the curry powder and cook for a further 2–3 minutes and then add the lemon juice.

6 Drain the cooked rice and stir into the spice and scallion mix. Add the fish and gently heat through.

7 Cut the eggs into quarters. Serve with the kedgeree and garnish with lemon halves.

GARLIC MUSSELS WITH CHORIZO

Ingredients

2 kg / 4½ lbs mussels

1 large onion

200 g / 7 oz chorizo

2 garlic cloves

Olive oil for frying

475 ml / 2 cups dry white wine

Pepper

Fresh parsley sprigs, to garnish

Method

Prep and cook time: 30 min

1 Clean the mussels by scrubbing the shells and pulling out any beards that are attached to them.

2 Roughly chop the onion. Remove the skin from the chorizo and roughly chop. Chop the garlic. Heat the olive oil in a large saucepan, add the onion and fry for 2–3 minutes, until softened.

3 Add the chorizo and cook for 2 minutes. Add the garlic and cook for a further 2–3 minutes.

4 Add the mussels, pour in the wine and season with pepper. Cover the pan, bring to the boil then cook over a medium heat for 5 minutes, until the mussels open.

5 Using a slotted spoon, discard any mussels that have not opened. Serve garnished with parsley.

TUNA SKEWERS WITH COUSCOUS

Ingredients

675 g / 1½ lb tuna fillet

2 cm / ¾ inch piece fresh ginger

Juice of 1 lemon

2 tbsp vegetable oil

Juice of 1 orange

2 tbsp honey

Lemon wedges, to garnish

For the couscous:

250 g / 1⅓ cups couscous

1 carrot

2 cm /1 inch piece fresh ginger

1 onion

2–3 tbsp toasted slivered (flaked) almonds

3–4 sprigs roughly chopped fresh parsley

2 tbsp butter

3 tbsp raisins

Juice of 1 orange

About 1 tbsp garlic oil

Salt and pepper

Method

Prep and cook time: 40 min plus 30 min marinating

1 Cut the fish into cubes. Peel and grate the ginger. Put the ginger, lemon juice and oil in a large bowl. Add the fish and put in the refrigerator for 30 minutes to marinate.

2 Thread the fish on to wooden skewers. Reserve the marinade.

3 To prepare the couscous, cook the couscous according to the packet instructions. Grate the carrot, grate the ginger and finely chop the onion.

4 Heat the butter in a saucepan, add the carrot, ginger and onion and cook until the onion is translucent. Add the slivered (flaked) almonds and raisins, stir in the orange juice and bring to the boil briefly. Add garlic oil to taste and season with salt and pepper.

5 Add the onion mixture and parsley to the couscous. Let stand then check the seasoning.

6 Meanwhile, preheat the broiler (grill) and broil (grill) the fish kebabs until tender, turning several times.

7 Put the reserved marinade and orange juice into a small pan. Bring to the boil and boil until reduced by half. Stir in the honey.

8 To serve, spoon the couscous on to warmed serving plates, add the fish kebabs and sprinkle over the sauce. Garnish with lemon wedges.

BABY OCTOPUS STEW

Ingredients

900 g / 2 lb baby octopus

2 garlic cloves

1 onion

1 fennel bulb

2 large potatoes

Two 400-g / 14-oz cans chopped tomatoes

2 tbsp olive oil

1 orange

1 liter / 4 cups water

8 saffron threads

½ tsp paprika

Salt and pepper

For the toasts:

1 roasted red bell pepper

2 garlic cloves

8 tbsp mayonnaise

½ tsp paprika

8 slices brown French bread

Method

Prep and cook time: 1 hr 20 min

1 Rinse the octopus and drain well. Remove the hard round beak at the base of the tentacles of each octopus.

2 Crush the garlic and chop the onion. Finely chop the fennel, reserving the tops. Slice the potatoes. Heat the oil in a large heavy-based saucepan, add the garlic, onion and fennel and fry until softened. Add the octopus, potatoes and tomatoes.

3 Use a vegetable peeler to remove the orange peel and add to the pan with the orange juice, water, saffron, paprika, 1 tsp salt and plenty of pepper.

4 Bring to a simmer, cover the pan and cook over a very low heat, stirring occasionally, for 45 minutes.

5 Uncover the pan and cook for a further 10 minutes or until the octopus is tender, when pierced with a knife, and the sauce is thick.

6 To make the toasts, chop the red pepper, discarding the core and seeds. Put the red pepper, garlic, mayonnaise and paprika into a food processor and blend until smooth. Spread on top of the warm toasted French bread. Serve the toasts with the stew, garnished with the fennel tops.

FISH CURRY

Ingredients

1 small can pineapple chunks

225 g / 8 oz cherry tomatoes

450 g / 1 lb white fish fillets

2 tbsp lemon juice

Salt and pepper

1 tbsp red curry paste

375 ml / 1²/₃ cups coconut milk

150 ml / ²/₃ cup plain yogurt

1 tsp corn starch (cornflour)

25 g / 1 cup shredded fresh basil

1–2 tbsp light soy sauce

8 chives, to garnish

For the rice:

Butter, for greasing

200 g / 1 cup basmati rice

Salt

Method

Prep and cook time: 40 min

1 Drain the pineapple chunks, reserving the juice in a jug. Roughly chop the pineapple. Slice the tomatoes in half.

2 Cut the fish into bite-size pieces, discarding any bones. Sprinkle the lemon juice over the top and season with salt and pepper.

3 Cook the rice according to the instructions on the packet. Lightly butter 4 individual molds.

4 Meanwhile, heat the oil in a wok, stir in the curry paste and fry briefly. Add the coconut milk, bring to the boil, and then simmer for 2 minutes. Stir in the pineapple chunks.

5 Mix the yogurt with the corn starch (cornflour) until smooth and add to the wok.

6 Pour in 150 ml / ²/₃ cup of the reserved pineapple juice and bring to the boil. Season with the soy sauce.

7 Add the fish pieces and tomatoes and bring to the boil. Cover, turn off the heat and allow to poach for 2–3 minutes. Stir in the basil.

8 Divide the rice equally into the prepared molds. Turn the rice out of the molds on to warmed plates. Serve the curry next to the rice and garnish with chives, if wished.

SMOKED MACKEREL PÂTÉ AND BEET RELISH

Ingredients

450 g / 1 lb smoked mackerel

225 g / 1 cup crème fraîche

2 tbsp ready-made creamed horseradish

Pepper

Slices of wholegrain bread, to serve

For the relish:

450 g / 1 lb beet (beetroot)

2 shallots

1 apple

4 tbsp brown sugar

4 tbsp red wine vinegar

2 tbsp lemon juice

About 3 tbsp red wine, if necessary

Salt

2 tbsp chopped fresh parsley

Method

Prep and cook time: 10 min plus 2 hrs chilling time
relish: 30 min plus 20 min marinating time

1 Put the mackerel, crème fraîche and creamed horseradish in a food processor and blend until smooth consistency. Season with pepper. Spoon into 4 small dishes and chill in the refrigerator for at least 2 hours.

2 To make the relish, peel and finely chop the beets (beetroot). Finely chop the shallots. Peel core and finely chop the apple. Put in a bowl and mix together.

3 Add the sugar, vinegar and lemon juice to the mixture and leave to marinate for about 20 minutes.

4 Put the mixture in a saucepan, bring to the boil and then simmer for 15–20 minutes, stirring occasionally, until cooked.

5 If necessary, add a little red wine but do not let the relish become too liquid. Season with salt, add the parsley and let cool.

6 Serve the pâté with the relish and slices of bread.

STUFFED SOLE

Ingredients

1 onion

1 garlic clove

1 roasted red bell pepper, drained

225 g / 8 oz baby spinach leaves

2 tbsp olive oil, plus some for greasing

150 g / ¾ cup long grain rice

Salt and pepper

4 sole fillets

Juice of 1 lemon, plus slices to garnish

1 tsp paprika

Watercress sprigs, to garnish

Method

Prep and cook time: 40 min

1 Preheat the oven to 190°C (375°F / Gas Mark 5). Grease an ovenproof dish. Chop the onion and crush the garlic. Chop the roasted red pepper.

2 Cook the rice according to the packet instructions.

3 Meanwhile, heat 1 tbsp of the olive oil in a large skillet (frying pan), add the onion and fry for about 5 minutes until softened. Add the garlic, pepper and spinach and cook for 2–3 minutes until the spinach has wilted. Season to taste with salt and pepper.

4 Drain the cooked rice and return to the pan. Add the vegetable mixture and stir together.

5 Lay the fish fillets in the prepared dish. Season with salt and pepper and pour over the lemon juice. Put 3 tablespoonfuls of the rice mixture in the middle of each fish fillet. Lift up the ends of the fish and secure with a toothpick (cocktail stick). Turn the fillets over so that the join is underneath.

6 Sprinkle over the paprika and drizzle over the remaining oil. Cook in the oven for 15 minutes or until the fish flakes. Garnish with watercress sprigs and lemon slices and serve with cooked vegetables.

FISH LASAGNA

Ingredients

Butter, for greasing

175 g / 6 oz lasagne sheets

225 g / 8 oz spinach

2 tomatoes

2 tbsp chopped fresh dill, plus extra to garnish

350 g / 12 oz white fish fillets

Salt

100 g / 1 cup grated Edam or Gouda cheese

For the sauce:

45 g / 3 tbsp butter

40 g / 1/3 cup all-purpose (plain) flour

350 ml / scant 1½ cups milk

Grated nutmeg

Salt and pepper

Method
Prep and cook time: 1 hr 30 min

1 Preheat the oven to 190°C (375°F / Gas Mark 5). Lightly grease a 33 x 23 cm / 13 x 9 inches ovenproof dish with butter.

2 Cook the lasagne sheets in a saucepan of boiling salted water according to the packet directions until tender but still with a slight bite. Drain well. Place, in a single layer, side by side, on paper towels (kitchen paper) to cool.

3 To make the sauce, melt the butter in a saucepan. Add the flour and cook until the flour begins to brown. Gradually add the milk, stirring all the time. Bring to the boil then reduce the heat and simmer for about 5 minutes, stirring occasionally. Season with nutmeg, salt and pepper.

4 Wash the spinach and put it in a large saucepan with only the water that clings to the leaves. Cover and cook over a high heat for 2–3 minutes. Drain into a sieve and squeeze out the excess water.

5 Blanch the tomatoes in a saucepan of boiling water. Remove the skins and then cut into wedges, discarding the seeds. Carefully stir the spinach, tomatoes and dill into the sauce.

6 Cut the fish fillets into bite-sized pieces. Season with salt. Place a single layer of lasagne sheets in the bottom of the ovenproof dish. Cover with half the fish and pour half the sauce on top. Add another layer of lasagne and the remaining fish. Pour over the remaining sauce. Sprinkle the grated cheese on top.

7 Bake in the oven for about 35 minutes until golden brown. Serve garnished with chopped dill.

Lasagne
m. Fisch

COD AND VEGETABLE GRATIN

Ingredients

1 tbsp butter, plus extra for greasing

4 cod fish fillets, each weighing
175 g / 6 oz

3 tbsp lemon juice

225 g / 8 oz carrots

225 g / 8 oz leeks

1 tbsp all-purpose (plain) flour

225 ml / 1 cup milk

¼ tsp sugar

¼ tsp grated nutmeg

1 tbsp medium hot mustard

½ tsp curry powder

Salt and pepper

2 tbsp crème fraîche

1–2 tbsp chopped fresh parsley

Method

Prep and cook time: 1 hr

1 Preheat the oven to 190°C (375°F / Gas Mark 5). Lightly grease an ovenproof dish with butter.

2 Sprinkle the fish with the lemon juice and leave to rest for 5–10 minutes. Finely slice the carrots and leeks.

3 Melt the butter in a saucepan. Stir in the flour and cook until the flour begins to brown. Using a whisk, gradually add the milk.

4 Bring the sauce to a boil and then simmer for 10 minutes. Add the sugar, nutmeg, mustard and curry and season to taste with salt and pepper. Remove from the heat and stir in the crème fraîche.

5 Put the carrots and leeks in the prepared dish, arrange the fish pieces on top and sprinkle with the parsley. Pour over the sauce.

6 Bake in the oven for 25–30 minutes until the fish is tender.

SEAFOOD RISOTTO WITH TROUT

Ingredients

2 garlic cloves

1 large onion

1 tomato

475 ml / 2 cups fish or vegetable broth (stock)

75 g / 6 tbsp butter

200 g / 1 cup risotto rice

150 ml / ²/₃ cup white wine

200 g / 7 oz peeled shrimp (prawns)

12 shelled mussels

4 trout fillets

4 tbsp grated Parmesan cheese

2 tbsp chopped fresh parsley, plus sprigs to garnish

1 lemon, sliced, to garnish

Method

Prep and cook time: 1 hr

1 Crush the garlic and chop the onion and tomato. Pour the broth (stock) into a saucepan and heat to simmering point.

2 Heat 50 g / 4 tbsp of the butter in a large heavy based saucepan. Add the garlic and onion and cook gently for 7 minutes until tender.

3 Stir in the rice and wine and bring to the boil, stirring gently until the wine is absorbed.

4 Over a medium heat and stirring constantly, add the stock, a little at time, allowing all the liquid to be absorbed after each addition.

5 After 15 minutes, add the shrimp (prawns), mussels and tomato to the risotto.

6 Meanwhile, heat the broiler (grill) and broil (grill) the trout fillets under a medium heat for about 10 minutes, turning once, until tender.

7 The risotto should be ready in about 20 minutes. When cooked, stir in the remaining butter, the Parmesan cheese and the parsley.

8 Serve with the grilled trout fillets and vegetables of your choice. Garnish with lemon slices and parsley sprigs.

POTATO PANCAKES AND SMOKED SALMON

Ingredients

115 g / 4 oz potatoes

Sea salt and pepper

2 eggs

7 tbsp milk

100 g / 1 cup all-purpose (plain) flour

25 g / 2 tbsp butter

8 slices smoked salmon

150 g / ²/₃ cup sour (soured) cream

Method

Prep and cook time: 40 min

1 Peel the potatoes, cut into large chunks and put in a saucepan of salted water. Cover, bring to the boil and simmer for about 20 minutes, until tender. Drain, return to the pan and mash until really smooth. Leave to cool for 2–3 minutes.

2 Beat the eggs and milk together in jug. Gradually stir the egg mixture into the potatoes until you have a smooth batter. Add the flour and season with salt and pepper.

3 Melt a knob of butter in a skillet (frying pan) and drop in a couple of ladlefuls of potato batter, spacing them well apart. The pancakes should be quite thick.

4 Fry the pancakes for 2–3 minutes each side until golden brown. Remove from the pan and keep warm while you cook the remaining mixture.

5 Season the sour cream with salt and pepper. Serve the pancakes with the smoked salmon and sour cream, sprinkled with sea salt, if wished.

SPAGHETTI WITH MUSSELS

Ingredients

1 kg / 2 lb 4 oz fresh mussels in shells

450 g / 1 lb cherry tomatoes

1 onion

4 garlic cloves

150 ml / ²/₃ cup white wine

Salt and pepper

450 g / 1 lb spaghetti

2 red chilies

2 tbsp olive oil

Salt and pepper

2 tbsp chopped fresh chives, to garnish

Method

Prep and cook time: 40 min

1 Clean the mussels by scrubbing the shells and pulling out any beards that are attached to them. Put in a large saucepan with a cupful of water. Cover with a tight fitting lid and cook for 3–4 minutes until the mussels open.

2 Using a slotted spoon, transfer to a bowl, discarding any mussels that have not opened. Strain the cooking juices and reserve.

3 Cut the tomatoes into quarters. Chop the onion and crush the garlic. Add the tomatoes, onion, garlic and wine to the pan, bring to the boil and simmer for 5 minutes.

4 Meanwhile, bring a large pan of salted water to the boil. Add the spaghetti and cook for about 10 minutes, or according to the packet instructions, until tender but still firm to the bite.

5 Finely slice the chilies, discarding the seeds. Add the chilies, oil, spaghetti and mussels to the tomato mixture and toss together. Season with salt and pepper and serve garnished with chopped chives.

Published by Transatlantic Press

First published in 2011

Transatlantic Press
38 Copthorne Road, Croxley Green, Hertfordshire WD3 4AQ

© Transatlantic Press

Images and Recipes by StockFood © The Food Image Agency

Recipes selected by Marika Kucerova, StockFood

A catalogue record for this book is available from the British Library.

ISBN: 978–1–907176–45–6

Printed in China

CONTENTS

Mirrorcollection

HEAD OF SYNDICATION & LICENSING: FERGUS MCKENNA
MIRRORPIX: mirrorpix.com 020 7293 3700
THANKS TO: JO SOLLIS, IVOR GAME, PAUL MASON, VITO INGLESE, MANJIT SANDHU, LISA TOMKINS, HOLLY BECKETT, JOHN MEAD

PRODUCED BY TRINITY MIRROR MEDIA, PO BOX 48, LIVERPOOL, L69 3EB
ISBN 9781910335383

MANAGING DIRECTOR: STEVE HANRAHAN
COMMERCIAL DIRECTOR: WILL BEEDLES
EXECUTIVE EDITOR: PAUL DOVE
EXECUTIVE ART EDITOR: RICK COOKE
SUB EDITING: ROY GILFOYLE, ADAM OLDFIELD
DESIGN & PRODUCTION: COLIN SUMPTER, COLIN HARRISON, CHRIS COLLINS, JULIE ADAMS
WRITERS: CHRIS BRERETON, ROBIN JAROSSI
PRINTED BY: WILLIAM GIBBONS

"I'M NOT A POP STAR, I'M NOT A MARVEL STAR, I'M NOT A FILM STAR…

I'M A BLACKSTAR

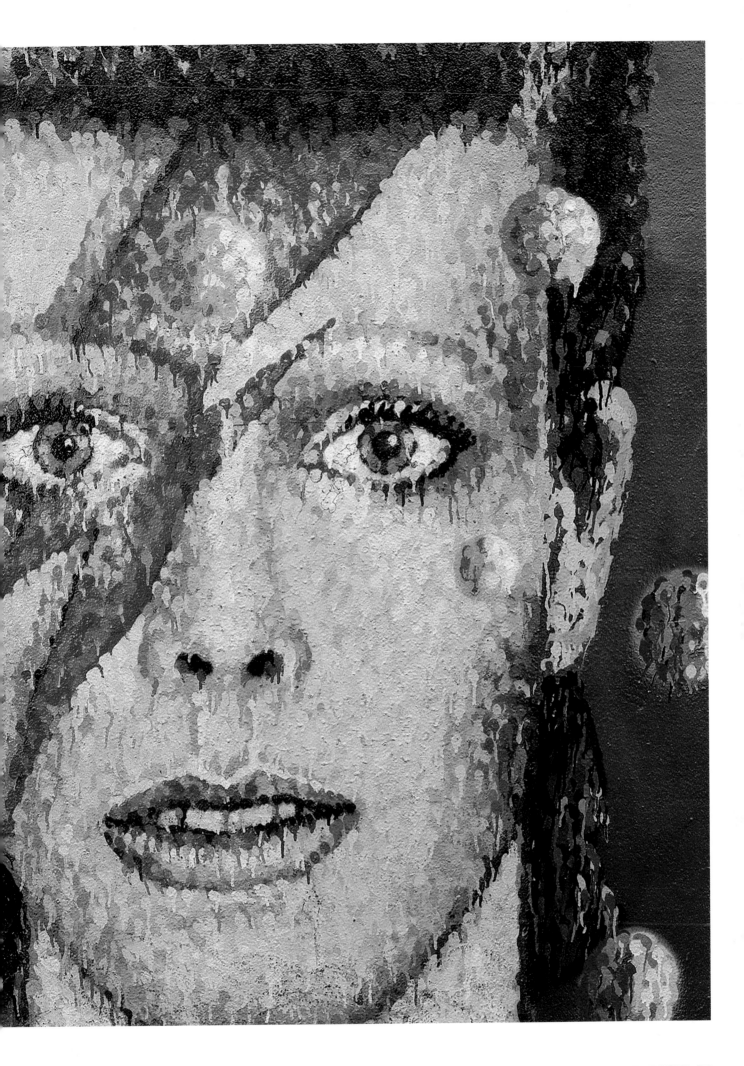

He was always ahead of the game, the trend, the consensus. And right at the end, he was even ahead of his own passing.

With Blackstar the artist-provocateur known as David Bowie managed to have the last word on his epic life and career with one final, sobering prediction. He sings on the track Lazarus: "Look up here, I'm in heaven... Look up here, man, I'm in danger, I've got nothing left to lose."

Before cancer claimed him a couple of days after his 69th birthday, the reviews for Blackstar described how audacious and oblique his latest album was. But few realised just how prescient and moving his lyrics would turn out to be.

Blackstar's final track, I Can't Give Everything Away, is generally seen as referring to Bowie's reluctance to be explicit about the meaning of his music throughout an amazing career. But who knew how emotionally charged this closing song really was?

"I know something is very wrong...
The blackout hearts, the flowered news,
With skull designs upon my shoes."

When news of his death was announced on Monday, January 11, we all caught up. The man that generations had followed through his dazzling and inspiring transformations for nearly 50 years was this time saying farewell.

Tony Visconti – long-term friend and producer on landmark albums from Space Oddity to Young Americans and ultimately Blackstar – said: "His death was no different from his life – a work of art. He made Blackstar for us, his parting gift."

And what an extraordinary gift. Acclaimed by critics on both sides of the Atlantic as "stunning" and "beautiful", Blackstar is yet another reinvention as the great pop adventurer switched to a modern jazzy and at times raucous new sound. Bowie drafted in New York musician Donny McCaslin's electro-acoustic trio to form the core of his backing group here, and it's quite a body-swerve from the guitar rock of his previous release, The Next Day.

Full of yearning and sonic surprises, his final studio album proved that Bowie could still upset expectations while storming the charts.

Has there ever been a superstar who has retained that spirit of restless experimentation while remaining so ultra-cool? Blackstar showed again that Bowie could never rest on his laurels or play safe. Not for him the knighthoods and mainstream blandness typical of rock aristocracy.

The sadness is that on Blackstar, Bowie is perhaps not hiding his meaning so much, and it's hard to miss the images of death now. As he sings these lines on the title track, we can guess at the dream-logic symbolism: "I'm not a pop star, I'm not a marvel star, I'm not a film star... I'm a blackstar."

So for one last time we are wrong-footed by Bowie on this gorgeous, unsettling record. It's a bold and even courageous sign-off.

Tony Visconti said after Bowie's death: "I knew for a year this was the way it would be. I wasn't, however, prepared for it. He was an extraordinary man, full of love and life. He will always be with us."

The mystique lives on.

ABOVE The third track, *Lazarus*, from Bowie's parting album *Blackstar* shows the singer retreating to a dark closet

RIGHT The video to *Lazarus* opens with Bowie lying in a hospital bed and the lyrics *"Look up here, I'm in heaven!"*

"HIS DEATH WAS NO DIFFERENT FROM HIS LIFE – A WORK OF ART. HE MADE BLACKSTAR FOR US, HIS PARTING GIFT

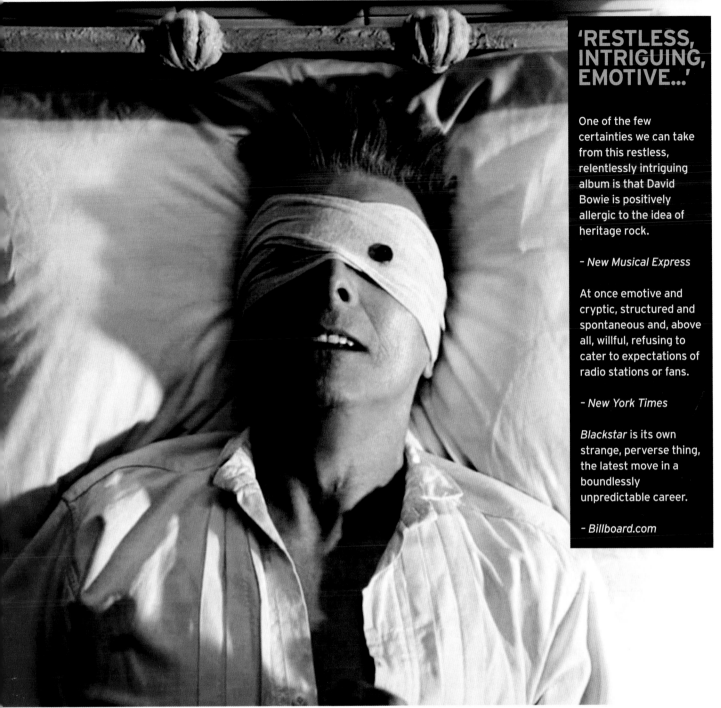

'RESTLESS, INTRIGUING, EMOTIVE...'

One of the few certainties we can take from this restless, relentlessly intriguing album is that David Bowie is positively allergic to the idea of heritage rock.

– New Musical Express

At once emotive and cryptic, structured and spontaneous and, above all, willful, refusing to cater to expectations of radio stations or fans.

– New York Times

Blackstar is its own strange, perverse thing, the latest move in a boundlessly unpredictable career.

– Billboard.com

LEFT *Lazarus* captures the anguish of a man struggling with his health

FAR LEFT Bowie's final music offering hits the shelves, bringing an end to a remarkable career and an extraordinary life

YOU ARE NOW AMONG
#HEROES

The disturbing news sent shockwaves around the world and prompted a flood of tributes. As Robin Jarossi writes, the reaction to his untimely death proved that David Bowie was many things to many people. Just as he would have wanted

What a shock. The starman has gone. It started with a message on his Facebook page: "David Bowie died peacefully today surrounded by his family after a courageous 18-month battle with cancer..."

The grim news was confirmed via a Tweet from his film director son, Duncan Jones – "Very sorry and sad to say it's true" – and the world woke on Monday, January 11, with the sobering feeling that the cultural landscape was suddenly less interesting. The much-loved Jean Genius of artistic rebellion and musical provocation had left the stage.

The outpouring of feeling was immediate and is ongoing.

Heads of government joined the tributes, pop royalty acknowledged their indebtedness to David Bowie, while millions of ordinary people took to Twitter and Facebook to recount their memories of growing up to the soundtrack of Ziggy Stardust and the Thin White Duke.

A "fearsome talent" is what Queen's Brian May, who played alongside Bowie on *Under Pressure*, called him. The Rolling Stones proclaimed him an "extraordinary artist" and "true original", while Sir Paul McCartney spoke of him as a "great star" who "played a very strong part in British musical history".

Spontaneous sadness saw flowers and messages placed outside of Bowie's New York

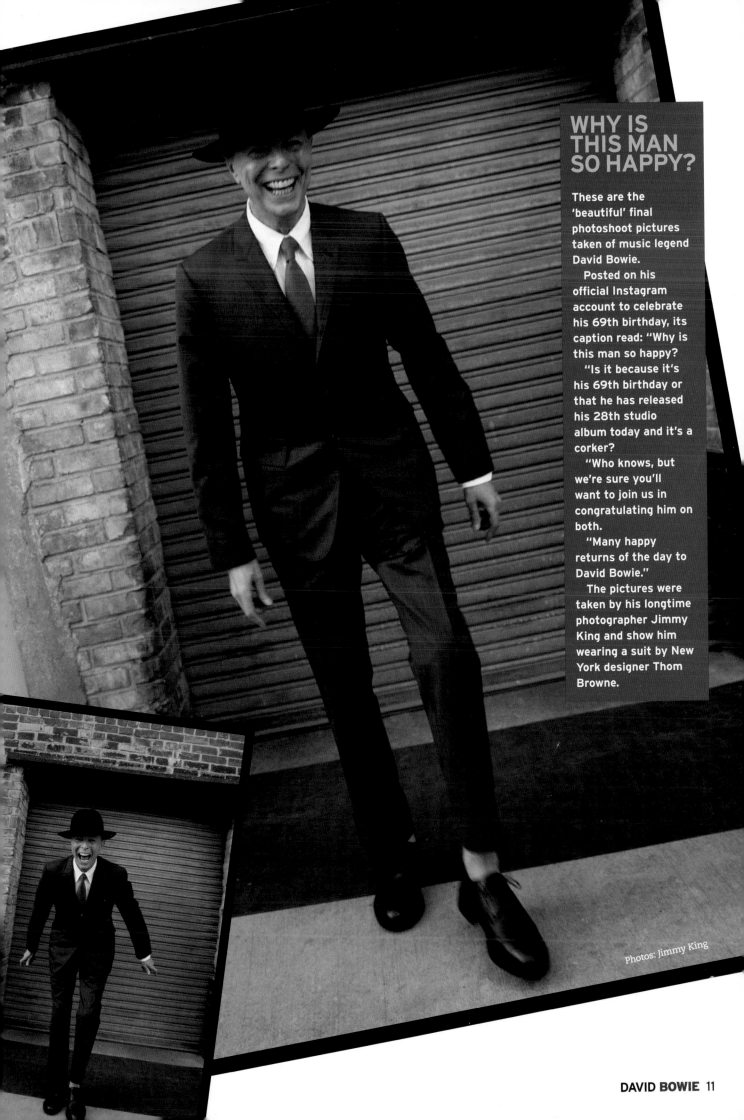

WHY IS THIS MAN SO HAPPY?

These are the 'beautiful' final photoshoot pictures taken of music legend David Bowie.

Posted on his official Instagram account to celebrate his 69th birthday, its caption read: "Why is this man so happy?

"Is it because it's his 69th birthday or that he has released his 28th studio album today and it's a corker?

"Who knows, but we're sure you'll want to join us in congratulating him on both.

"Many happy returns of the day to David Bowie."

The pictures were taken by his longtime photographer Jimmy King and show him wearing a suit by New York designer Thom Browne.

Photos: Jimmy King

home, while thousands of Londoners staged an impromptu outdoor party a few streets away from where he was born in Brixton.

He had allies in unexpected places. The Vatican's newspaper L'Osservatore Romano praised him in an article entitled Bowie: Never Banal (which must be one of the greatest understatements ever made about him), and Archbishop of Canterbury Justin Welby remembered his music as his "personal soundtrack".

There were fond salutations from old friends, including most remarkably the German government: "Good-bye, David Bowie. You are now among #Heroes. Thank you for helping to bring down the #wall."

In 1987 he played a concert in West Berlin that could be heard in the East. He sent best wishes in German to those listening over the Wall, sang Heroes and caused riots in the East, helping to change the mood in the totalitarian half of the city. Two years later, the Wall fell.

Tearing down barriers was something Bowie also did on a personal level for millions who fell under his spell.

Listening to the outlandish dude from Brixton banging out Rebel Rebel gave many teens a little swagger the next day as they went to school. Seeing him drape his arm around guitarist Mick Ronson on Top Of The Pops in 1972 and proclaiming his bisexuality that same year no doubt gave many sexually unsure youngsters some confidence to be themselves.

He was born in 1947 in Brixton, London, as David Robert Jones, eventually changing his name to Bowie to avoid the shadow of the Monkees' Davy Jones.

The man who would become the master cultural shapeshifter tried many different guises during the 1960s in his bid for stardom. He played the sax in The Kon-rads, studied mime, made novelty records, joined an R&B band and tried to be a folkie.

His first album, David Bowie, was released in 1967 on the same day as Sgt Pepper's Lonely Hearts Club Band. The record reached No3 in the charts but Bowie still failed to click as a star. The single Space Oddity came in 1969, which finally gave him a commercial success.

His first distinctive albums were The Man Who Sold The World, followed by Hunky Dory in 1971.

But when he finally made a real splash, it was a tidal wave.

The following year he released The Rise And Fall Of Ziggy Stardust and The Spiders From Mars. Containing several classic Bowie masterpieces - Starman, Moonage Daydream, Ziggy Stardust - it was like nothing else on the pop scene and made him an international star.

Moreover, Bowie turned himself into the flame-haired, tight-trousered persona of Ziggy onstage, dismaying parents while thrilling their children.

The image changed as the classic albums shook up the 1970s – Aladdin Sane, Diamond Dogs, Station To Station, Low, Heroes.

Now that Bowie had tapped into his talent he was everywhere, producing the classic album Transformer for Lou Reed in New York, giving Mott The Hoople their biggest hit with All The Young Dudes, teaming up with Lulu and even Bing Crosby. Later landmark collaborations would include hit singles with Queen and Mick Jagger.

The "otherness" projected by his music made him the ideal choice to play the lead in Nic Roeg's 1976 sci-fi movie The Man Who Fell To Earth. Further roles followed in Just A Gigolo, Merry Christmas, Mr Lawrence and as a vampire lover in The Hunger.

His most commercially rewarding time came during the New Romantic era of the early 1980s with the release of Scary Monsters and particularly Let's Dance in 1983, which followed on from his acclaimed but more serious Berlin trilogy of albums (Low, Heroes and Lodger). Let's Dance was No1 in the UK and US, and its hit singles included the title track along with Modern Love and China Girl.

At this time a new generation of stars were flourishing who certainly followed Bowie's lead in challenging the mainstream with their music and image. Boy George, Gary Numan, Morrissey, Phil Oakey, Kate Bush and Adam Ant were all among Bowie's creative offspring.

ABOVE David Bowie in London in August 1981. The Ziggy Stardust stage may have been over by then but three more decades of critical acclaim were to follow

" IT'S ALMOST HARD TO BELIEVE THIS INSPIRATIONAL INNOVATOR WOULD DO ANYTHING AS PREDICTABLE AS DYING

Photo: Vantagenews.co.uk

Celebrated by this time as a bold innovator in music and fashion, Bowie's chart popularity had peaked. This commercial period, which included one of his least satisfactory albums, *Tonight* in 1984, did not thrill him artistically. His hard-rocking quartet *Tin Machine* followed but failed to win over critics or a large following.

Later albums including *Black Tie White Noise* (1992), *Outside* (1995), *Earthling* (1997) and *Heathen* (2002) showed Bowie rediscovering his creative spark and enjoying chart success and critical praise.

His health finally halted his career as a live performer. Having once smoked 60 cigarettes a day and been a coke addict many years before, he collapsed at a concert in Scheesel, Germany, in 2004, and he required emergency surgery on a blocked artery. His last live show was with Alicia Keys at a New York fundraiser in 2006.

His final years of apparent seclusion living in the Big Apple with wife Iman and daughter Lexi did harbour one last surprise from the star as he secretly worked away in the studio. He finished with the flourish of two final acclaimed albums, 2013's startling, unannounced *The Next Day* and January 2016's *Blackstar*, released on his 69th birthday.

And once again Ziggy has everyone talking and listening, wondering about the messages of foreboding in *Blackstar* and the extent to which he stage-managed his passing.

The shock is still palpable. It's almost hard to believe that this inspirational innovator would ever do anything as boringly predictable as dying.

But Bowie's music and career have given us Golden Years galore. That's still something to celebrate...

Photo: Vantagenews.co.uk

LEFT Attending the premiere of the musical *Lazarus* in December 2015, at New York Theatre Workshop. The musical features Bowie songs and tells the story of a human-looking alien who comes to Earth. Bowie was greeted by a legion of fans on his final public appearance

THE EARLY YEARS

After starting his career in music as Davy Jones, it didn't take long for his characteristic flamboyance to shine through. And he was comfortable enough in the public eye to allow the cameras to capture a family stroll alongside wife Angie and baby boy Zowie

BBC TELEVISI

'BE FAIR TO LONG HAIR'

Singer Davy Jones is pictured here outside the BBC television centre in March 1965, where he and his band were to perform *I Pity The Fool* on the BBC show 'Gadzooks! It's All Happening'.

The show's producer, Barry Langford, insisted that Bowie cut his hair, which he refused to do and organised demonstrations at the BBC with banners like 'Be Fair To Long Hair'.

The group were later allowed to appear on the show with the condition that if they got complaints, the band's fee would go to charity. No complaints were received.

PACKING A PUNCH

Bowie attended Bromley Technical High School and that was where he suffered the eye injury that added so much extra allure to his already elusive image.

Bowie, or Jones as he was still called – was punched in the face by schoolfriend George Underwood as they fought over a girl. That left Bowie with one blue retina and one brown. Bowie held no grudges though and remained a good friend with Underwood throughout his life.

ABOVE LEFT Bowie when he was still known as David Jones in March 1965
ABOVE RIGHT A smart looking Bowie smiles for the cameras in 1970
ABOVE Bowie's unusual dress sense on display at his home in Beckenham, Kent, in April 1971
OPPOSITE Bowie, wife Angie and baby son Zowie take part in a 1971 photoshoot

RIGHT Bowie with
wife Angie and
three-week-old son
Zowie going for a walk
in June 1971

LEFT Bowie continues to pout for the cameras alongside Angie and Zowie

BELOW A classic 70s look from behind

BOTTOM Guitars are strewn around Bowie's home in the final shot of a 1971 photoshoot

ODD FACT

The now renamed David Bowie released his first album, *David Bowie*, in 1967 but his first major hit came two years later with 1969's *Space Oddity*. It was a song that connected well with the psychedelic era and when Neil Armstrong and Buzz Aldrin landed on the moon in Apollo 11 in July 1969, the BBC used the music as the main theme on their coverage.

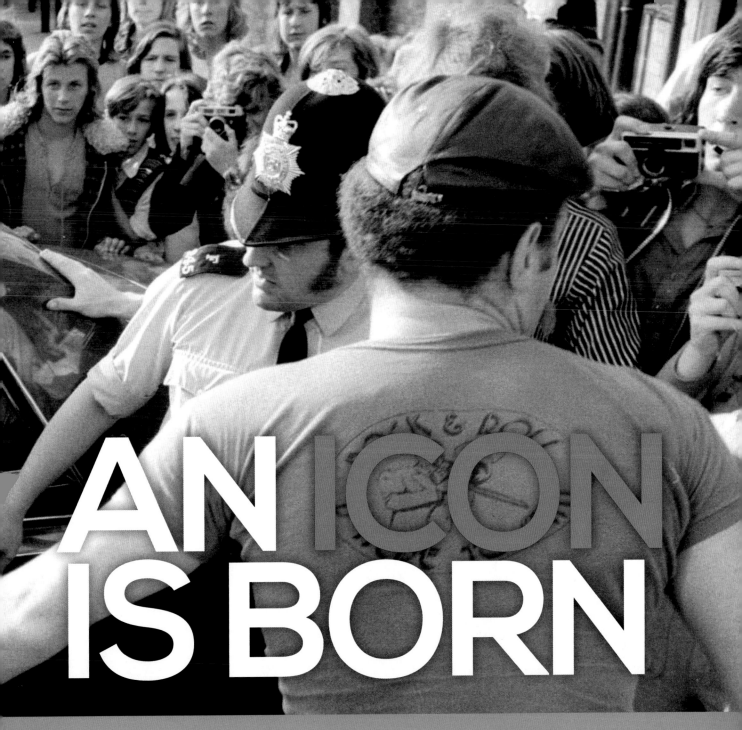

AN ICON IS BORN

If Bowie had chased fame in the 1960s, then fame more than chased him during the decade to come. The 1970s was perhaps the most iconic, creative and unusual of Bowie's career. After marrying first wife Angie in March 1970, he went on later that year to release *The Man Who Sold The World*; an album that still sells heavily across the globe. It also announced a new, ethereal Bowie – an androgynous image – neither male or female – that would be developed ever further as the decade progressed

'TOMORROW BELONGS TO THOSE WHO CAN HEAR IT COMING'

TUNS OF TALENT IN BECKENHAM

There are many iconic places in cultural history but the Three Tuns pub in Beckenham is not a place you would immediately recognise as the home of one of music's most iconic transformations.

However, it was here that Bowie first considered experimenting with his Ziggy Stardust persona, a flamboyant, larger than life alien rock star who Bowie inhabited entirely.

He wasn't a character, Ziggy was a persona that Bowie lived, utterly.

The record *The Rise and Fall of Ziggy Stardust and the Spiders From Mars* in 1972 was a concept album that propelled Bowie to the top of the musical world; a position he was never to leave.

ABOVE Bowie performing on stage at Brighton Dome theatre in May 1973

LEFT Bowie flamboyantly dressed in 1974

MIDDLE AND LEFT Bowie leaning out of a railway carriage of the Paris boat train at Victoria station in July 1973

OPPOSITE Bowie was never scared to shock fans or critics with his outrageous, out-of-this-world outfits

CONSUMED BY A DRUG ADDICTION

As the 70s progressed, and as Bowie's popularity on both sides of the Atlantic grew, he found himself in increasing private turmoil, prompted by a colossal cocaine habit.

Bowie could snort vast amounts of the drug and he apparently could not remember his 1973 album *Pin Ups* because he was constantly under the influence.

One look at the photos of Bowie during the decade show a stick-thin artist, racked by addiction problems and he later admitted that his cocaine problem nearly killed him.

RIGHT Bowie at the premiere of *Live and Let Die*, Odeon Leicester Square, London, July 1973

ABOVE Bowie is presented with six discs from RCA Records to mark the occasion of having six albums in the charts in December 1973

ABOVE LEFT Bowie and friends, including Lulu, Ringo Starr (left) and Cat Stevens (right centre) at Bowie's famous 'Last Supper' party at London's Cafe Royal, to commemorate the last show ever done by 'Ziggy Stardust and the Spiders from Mars' which had taken place at the Hammersmith Odeon the day before in July 1973

ABOVE (left to right) Lou Reed, Mick Jagger and David Bowie share a joke at the Cafe Royal party

BERLIN CALLING

In 1976, Bowie moved to Berlin from Los Angeles in a bid to escape the drug-fuelled hedonism of his life in America.

The move to Germany was inspired and would help Bowie produce some of his most iconic and memorable tracks. Indeed, he wrote *Heroes* while living in the city and claimed the track was inspired by a couple he used to watch on a daily basis.

"They'd meet at a little bench right under the Berlin Wall, where guards are posted at 20 yard intervals. Of all the places in West Berlin, why meet next to a guard's turret right by the Wall?

"I wondered if there was something illicit about their affair and they felt they were being heroic by meeting there. I went to Berlin because it provided the friction I needed for my work."

The city certainly brought the best out of Bowie and the way that Germany mourned his death underlines the fact that Berlin loved Bowie as much as Bowie loved Berlin.

ABOVE 'Ziggy Stardust' in concert in Scotland in May 1973

OPPOSITE Bowie at the Empire Pool, Wembley, as part of his 'Isolar' tour in May 1976

LEFT, BOTTOM LEFT AND MIDDLE Bowie performing at Wembley in June 1978

BOTTOM RIGHT Ever the showman, Bowie struts his stuff, again at Wembley but this time in May 1976

OPPOSITE Bowie pictured in a scene from the film *Just A Gigolo* during production in Berlin in February 1978

"LIKE A BISEXUAL ALLEYCAT"

If Bowie's appetite for drugs was vast, it was nothing compared to his sexual demands, and ex-wife Angie recently described Bowie as "a bisexual alleycat".

Nobody was off limits for Bowie – male or female – and he and Angie were late for their wedding in 1970 because they'd indulged in a threesome that morning! It was all part of the Bowie mystery and allure though. His list of notable sexual partners runs into the hundreds, including Elizabeth Taylor, Marianne Faithfull, Bianca Jagger, Susan Sarandon and, perhaps most famously, an alleged fling with Rolling Stones lead singer Mick Jagger.

In 1976, Bowie told Playboy magazine that he was bisexual but then denied that during the 1980s.

Whatever the truth, Bowie's bed-hopping in the '70s and '80s have added another angle to a legendary life – where fact and fiction have merged to create a man many loved, but few really knew.

ABOVE Bowie arrives home at Victoria Station, London, during his 'Isolar 'tour in May 1976

BELOW, LEFT AND RIGHT Posing for the media in 1978   MIDDLE On stage in 1976

'FOR MANY YEARS BERLIN HAD APPEALED TO ME AS A SORT OF SANCTUARY'

ABOVE Bowie performs at Wembley in May 1976

LEFT Greeting fans with a smile from a Mercedes convertible as he is welcomed back to London in May 1976

THE MAN WHO FELL INTO ACTING

David Bowie's talents extended further than the recording studio or the concert stage...

From Pontius Pilate to the Elephant Man and from Zoolander to Labyrinth, it is important not to forget the films and acting performances that David Bowie undertook throughout his career.

While nobody would suggest that Bowie's film career matched his musical endeavours - in either creativity or popular acclaim - his willingness to appear on the silver screen underlines his experimental ambition.

As a musician, Bowie cannot really be defined by a set of genres - he transcended pop and rock'n'roll and made a brand of music that was his and his alone.

And, at times, he also played characters in films and on stage who nobody else could have even attempted.

That was never truer than in his first big movie role in 1976 in The Man Who Fell To Earth - the story of an alien who visits Earth in a bid to try and save his dying home planet, a planet desperately in need of water. As Thomas "Tommy" Jerome Newton, Bowie delivers a wonderfully spooky performance, perfectly capturing the essence of his role.

Bowie continued to display his ethereal side in The Hunger in 1983 as he played a vampire racing around New York, trying to defy time while enlisting the help of Susan Sarandon to try and stay alive.

ABOVE Bowie surrounded by the three leading lady stars in the film *Just A Gigolo* in 1978. Left to right are Maria Schell, Kim Novak and Sydne Rome

LEFT Bowie prepares for a scene during filming of *The Man Who Fell to Earth* in July 1975

Later that year, Bowie played Major Jack 'Strafers' Celliers in *Merry Christmas Mr. Lawrence*, a film that included a homoerotic relationship with the commander of the WW2 POW camp that Bowie's character had been sent to. Bowie's range and acting talents were never on better display than in this film which showed a different side to life inside the brutal Japanese camps.

The film roles kept coming such as Absolute Beginners (1986), Basquiat (1996) and The Prestige (2006) plus cameos in Zoolander (2001), Twin Peaks: Fire Walk With Me (1992), Yellowbeard (1983), The Last Temptation of Christ (1988) and even a voiceover on Spongebob SquarePants (2007). However, no discussion of Bowie's acting ability is complete without a mention of his most famous and popular role.

Kids across the globe were both terrified and enraptured by Bowie's performance in Labyrinth in 1986. Bowie stole the show as the evil Jareth the Goblin King, in the fantasy film of the decade, a rollercoaster ride through a mystical story that was as scary as it was entertaining.

Labyrinth is the first film that Bowie fans will think of when they consider his acting roles but, as these photos show, his versatility and enjoyment of acting were there for all to see.

ABOVE Showing his versatility as an actor in New York City in 1982
BELOW Director David Hemmings shows Bowie how to tango during the shooting of *Just A Gigolo* in February 1978

MAIN AND INSET
Bowie played John
Merrick in *The Elephant
Man* on Broadway, New
York, in 1980

GOIN' STRAIGHT

In the 1980s, Bowie transformed himself again, from an uber-experimental showman to a sleeker commercial musician. He called this decade his 'Phil Collins years', a wry tribute to Collins's ability to make big money filling stadiums

MAIN On stage at the Birmingham NEC on the 'Serious Moonlight Tour' in June 1983

INSET Bowie performs at the Milton Keynes Bowl a month later

OPPOSITE A typically theatrical concert in full 'swing' at Wembley

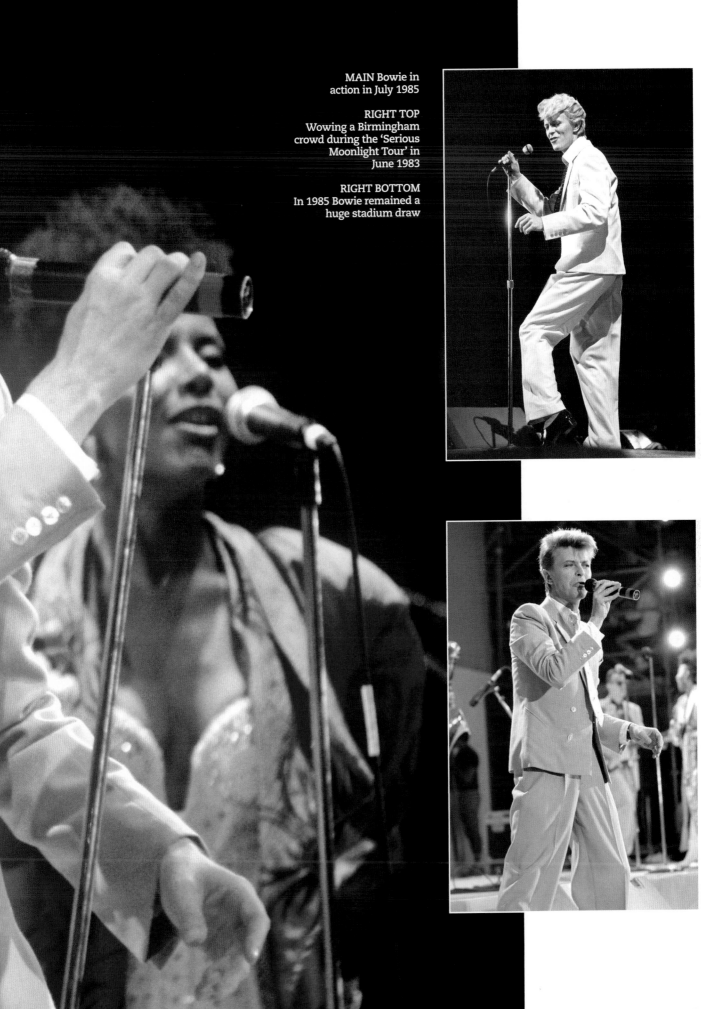

MAIN Bowie in action in July 1985

RIGHT TOP Wowing a Birmingham crowd during the 'Serious Moonlight Tour' in June 1983

RIGHT BOTTOM In 1985 Bowie remained a huge stadium draw

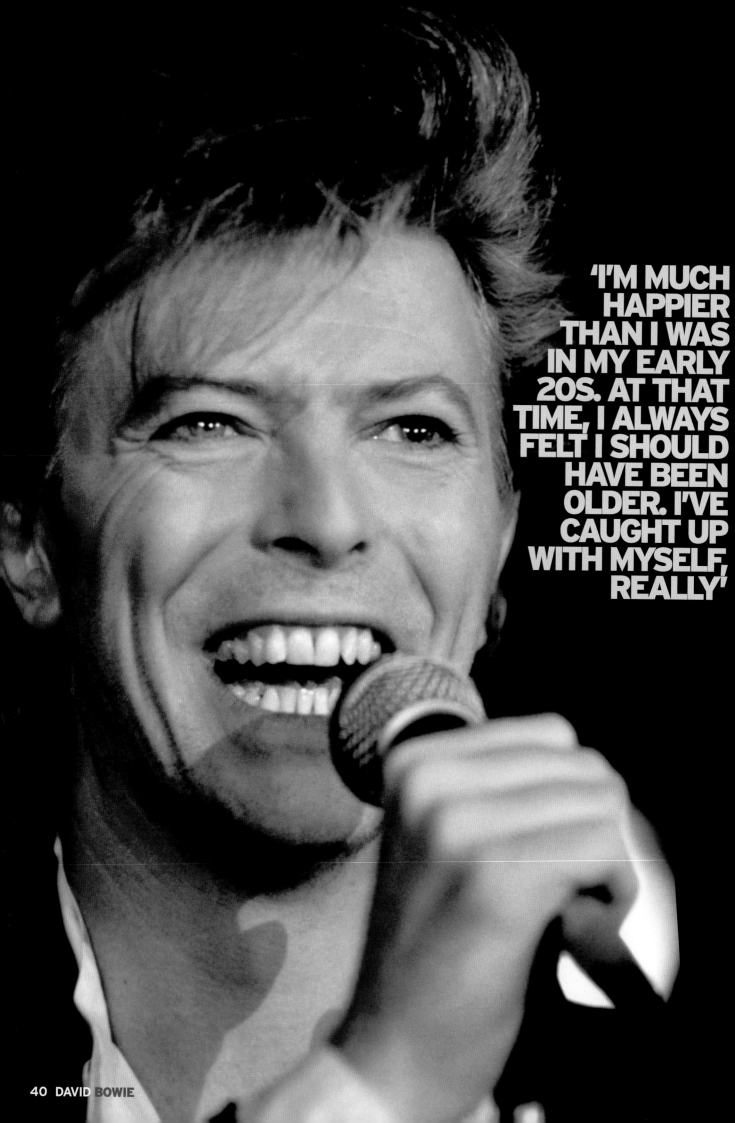

'I'M MUCH HAPPIER THAN I WAS IN MY EARLY 20S. AT THAT TIME, I ALWAYS FELT I SHOULD HAVE BEEN OLDER. I'VE CAUGHT UP WITH MYSELF, REALLY'

OPPOSITE AND TOP LEFT, RIGHT Bowie singing at a London press conference as he announced his world tour in March 1987

BOTTOM LEFT Two British icons side by side.
Bowie laughs at a Paul McCartney joke in July 1985

BOTTOM RIGHT Bowie in typical pose on stage during his 1987 'Glass Spider' tour

On June 23, 1987, Bowie kept Sunderland's Roker Park enchanted for hours, performing in front of 25,000 adoring fans in the north-east of England as part of his 'Glass Spider' tour

ALL Bowie's showmanship, outfits and stage energy all continued to sparkle throughout the 1980s as he filled huge stadiums across the globe. For a man who once claimed to be painfully shy, his transformation during the decade into a performer comfortable enough to entertain thousands was a further development in a career that had already brought plenty of highs

THE RESTLESS SUPERSTAR

As the decade drew to a close, it became clear that Bowie was already thinking about his next career move. The chameleon was ready to change his colours again.

He said: "Being shoved into the top 40 scene was an unusual experience. It was great I'd become accessible to a huge audience, but not terribly fulfilling.

"It seemed so easy. It was cheers from the word go.

"You know how to get a reaction – play *Changes*, *Golden Years* and they'd be up on their feet. You get the reaction, take the money and run away. It seemed too easy. I didn't want to do that again."

SHARING HIS TALENT WITH FRIENDS

David Bowie's longevity, impact and sustained brilliance over four decades means his musical legacy is set in stone. Fans will forever think of him as the main attraction on any stage he ever graced, a preening peacock at the top of his game.

However, it should not be forgotten how often Bowie was willing to share the limelight with other artists.

In fact, few, if any, other major musical stars of the past 50 years can be said to have collaborated more, or with more spectacular results.

Everybody from John Lennon to Lulu to Freddie Mercury shared a microphone with The Thin White Duke.

Where to start? There are almost too many to mention.

Fans of a certain vintage are perhaps likely to be drawn automatically to Bowie's version of Martha and the Vandella's *Dancing in the Streets* with the Rolling Stones' Mick Jagger in 1985.

The two UK music gods linked up in London's Docklands to record a version of the song for Live Aid, helping to raise millions in the process.

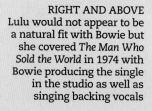

RIGHT AND ABOVE
Lulu would not appear to be a natural fit with Bowie but she covered *The Man Who Sold the World* in 1974 with Bowie producing the single in the studio as well as singing backing vocals

Bowie and Tina Turner, a fellow 1980s music giant, duet at the NEC in Birmingham as part of Turner's *Private Dancer* our in March, 1983. Bowie joined Turner late on to sing *Tonight* and *Let's Dance*

Tina Turner, another 80s superstar, also benefited from Bowie's presence as he recorded *Tonight* with Turner in 1984 as well as also turning up on her *Private Dancer* tour to surprise audiences with a duet of the song.

Then there is *Under Pressure*, Bowie and Queen's collaboration in 1981, a song that was so successful it ended Queen's six-year long wait for a No.1 single (their previous No.1 being a certain Bohemian Rhapsody).

For a man who constantly lived on the edge, the most memorable duet of Bowie's career came in 1977 on Bing Crosby's Merrie Olde Christmas show.

To see the controversial king of British reinvention singing *Little Drummer Boy* alongside Crosby, the epitome of cardigan-clad American convention, remains as surreal today as it was then. Bowie claimed he only went on the show to please his Crosby-loving mum and as excuses go, it is as valid as any other!

Annie Lennox, Lulu, Iggy Pop, Lou Reed, Arcade Fire and Pink Floyd's David Gilmour have also all shared a stage with Bowie, and him appearing from the shadows of the stage to help out

with Gilmour's version of *Comfortably Numb* in 2009 at London's Royal Albert Hall is perhaps the highlight.

It was not just in front of the microphone either. Lennon, by then living in New York following the end of the Beatles, co-wrote Fame for the *Young Americans* album with Bowie in 1975, helping him to his first top spot on the Billboard 100 while an exhibition of Bowie in the Victoria and Albert Musuem in London in 2013 underlined his willingness to work with artists and venues across a wide spectrum of interests.

Looking back, it appeared that everybody wanted to work with Bowie, knowing that his undoubted quality would rub off on them. It is to his credit that he was so generous with his time, and genius, to leave behind so many memorable duets.

ABOVE Bowie singing *Under Pressure* with Annie Lennox at the Freddie Mercury Tribute Concert at Wembley in 1992

TOP RIGHT AND OPPOSITE Bowie was one of the biggest artists to help out Bob Geldof's Live Aid project in 1985 and he recorded *Dancing in the Street* with Mick Jagger in a bid to raise millions for starving children in Africa

IMAN OF INFLUENCE

Bowie had managed to wean himself off hard drugs during the late 1980s and meeting supermodel wife Iman in 1990 transformed his life. Iman was the inspiration Bowie needed to remain clean and sober as he continued to record, perform and inspire a new generation of artists

Bowie was on fine form as he performed at the Mayfair club in Newcastle in November 1991

IN IMAN'S WORDS

Bowie spoke often of his love for his wife but it was always clear that Iman was just as happy as her husband was.

She said: "With David, I'm never bored and he pushes me, you know? He's brought all my dormant passions about politics and creating to life.

"I'd put that part of me aside when I modelled but he's just encouraged me. I've learned so much from him. He's my rock."

In full voice at The
Riverside in Newcastle
in 1997

The 1990s saw a more relaxed Bowie on stage as his stamina, showmanship and crowd interaction all improved. He appeared to become more comfortable as a performer and his vast and popular back catalogue had fans well and truly gripped

ABOVE Bowie in action at the Newcastle Arena in December 1995
LEFT, MIDDLE With Eric Clapton at the 1995 Q Music Awards in London

LEFT The wry smile says it all. Bowie thoroughly enjoying himself on his Sound and Vision Tour in Birmingham in March 1990

BELOW Bowie and Iman in 1995. Their marriage and secure lifestyle became Bowie's happiest achievement

Bowie on stage in Aberdeen in November 1995

WEB MASTER

It wasn't just in the world of music where Bowie was one step ahead.

In an online chat with the Mirror in October 1999 he revealed that he was also a pioneer of the cyberspace revolution.

Bowie used email as early as 1983, was the first to release a single on the internet and his hit album *Hours* was available online 10 days before it hit the shops.

Bowie, then 52, said: "If I were 19 now, I would bypass music and go straight on to the internet. That's what attracted me to music in the first place – the idea that you could change things.

"Music doesn't have the same revolutionary subversive battle cry that it had when it was still regarded as anti-establishment."

Bowie revealed that he had to cut down his time on the internet as wife Iman wasn't happy with the amount of time he spent surfing.

While he said that some of his contemporaries weren't aware of their own email address, he revealed that he was in regular email contact with Goldie and Flea from the Red Hot Chili Peppers.

LEAVING A MODERN MARK

In recent times, everybody from The Killers to U2 to Lady Gaga have been influenced by Bowie's musicianship and the way he fused music, art and acting together into one unforgettable package.

Lady Gaga said of Bowie: "He's sort of like an alien prince. He still runs my universe as well, like, every morning I wake up and I think, 'What would Bowie do?'"

U2 frontman Bono said: "He introduced us to Berlin and Hansa Studios, to collaborating with Brian Eno. What Elvis meant to America, Bowie meant to Britain and Ireland."

'I'M NOW PROBABLY TRUER TO MY REAL NATURE THAN I'VE EVER BEEN. AND IT'S WONDERFUL'

To celebrate his 60th birthday back in 2007, an older, wiser and happier David Bowie gave the Daily Mirror an exclusive interview on the troubled life he had left behind

JUST a few days ago a distinguished looking Englishman walked into a family bookshop in Greenwich Village, New York, and politely requested help in choosing a children's novel.

Putting a copy of the French children's classic Madeline on the counter, he asked the owner if the story was "absolutely suitable" for his six-year-old daughter, before handing over a credit card bearing the name Mr David R Jones.

In rock 'n' roll terms, this is not an anecdote that would ever add to the great David Bowie myth.

But for a superstar who took sex, drugs and rock 'n' roll to the extreme (and then some), it says everything about the man who turns 60 on Monday – and has finally found happiness as a father and family man.

Unlike his contemporary – and alleged former lover – Mick Jagger, Bowie's 60th birthday isn't being marked by a series of parties full of sexy models and expensive gifts.

Instead, Bowie will spend the day at home in his high-rise apartment in downtown Manhattan.

His six-year-old daughter, Lexi, has made him a card, while Iman, his wife of almost 15 years, plans to cook his favourite dish, shepherd's pie.

Then the man formerly known as Ziggy Stardust will curl up on the sofa with Lexi to watch their favourite cartoon, SpongeBob SquarePants.

Bowie's 35-year-old director son, Duncan Jones, (formerly Zowie Bowie) is due over in the evening along with Iman's daughter, Zulehka, 28, for a family celebration.

"David is going to be 60 but he is not freaking out about it," admits Iman. "I guess that's because he's happy. We just lead a very simple family life."

This was not the future Bowie predicted for himself back when even his image was banned from American record albums for being too wild.

Born in Brixton, south London, the young David Jones did anything he could to escape normality. After learning to play the saxophone at his school in Bromley, Kent, he realised that the only way to get noticed was by being the lead singer in a band. "I had a repulsive need to be more than human," he says.

Tall, thin and with two different coloured eyes – the result of a playground fight – he was the first of his generation to understand that image was key.

Before Madonna even existed, Bowie was the ultimate pop chameleon, morphing from Ziggy Stardust to Aladdin Sane to The Thin White Duke, outraging the public with his exotic make-up, subversive lyrics and talking openly about his sexual affairs with both men and women.

"Actually, back then I lied," he says now. "I said I was gay when actually I was bisexual." When he married Cypriot-born Angie Barnett, she famously complained that he spent too much time in bed with Jagger.

Bowie admits that as his fame grew, his behaviour spiralled out of control as his addiction to drink and cocaine took over his gilded life.

He moved to Los Angeles in the '70s and spent most of his time being driven around in limos, snorting industrial quantities of cocaine and pushing the envelope of decadence.

"The night I met Iggy Pop and Lou Reed we all sat at a table together in Max's Kansas City not speaking. We were all out-cooling each other. It was all about attitude," he recalls.

"A lot of it was to do with me trying to function behind what was an extremely shy personality. Like most people who get deeply involved in drugs, I felt it helped me to break out of my inhibitions but it just throws you into a quagmire of emotional hell."

He adds: "It was an awful period. I couldn't even eat. I weighed just 95lbs and it still amazes me I managed to survive.

"The only escape for me was to finish my association with cocaine."

ABOVE
Bowie admits that, at his peak, the fame that followed his success led to his behaviour spiralling out of control

"IT WAS AN AWFUL PERIOD. I COULDN'T EVEN EAT. I WEIGHED JUST 95LBS AND IT STILL AMAZES ME I MANAGED TO SURVIVE

Throughout the '70s he released hit after hit album, from *Ziggy Stardust* to *Diamond Dogs* to *Young Americans* to *Low* and *Scary Monsters*. Coke addiction gave way to alcoholism following a move to Berlin in 1977. And the '80s saw his most commercially successful time when on the back of *Let's Dance*, he became a true stadium superstar in what he now calls his "Phil Collins" period.

But personal happiness had eluded him until he met Somali-born supermodel Iman.

They were brought together by a mutual friend at a dinner party in LA in October 1990. Eighteen months later, Bowie proposed on a boat trip through Paris and they wed in Florence in April 1992.

It was Iman's subsequent struggle to conceive that changed the superstar's life. She went through IVF several times before giving birth to Lexi in August 2000.

Since then, Bowie has turned his back on his celebrity lifestyle.

He bought a 64-acre country retreat in upstate New York – where he goes to write and paint – and sold off his "rock star" homes in Switzerland and Mustique.

Two years ago, after a heart operation, he decided to cut down on work again.

"David really does lead the simple life," says a friend. "He's at home a lot. He walks Lexi to school and picks her up. He's totally vice free – the last thing to go were the fry-ups and cigarettes – which he gave up four years ago. But having known David for four decades, I can say he's happier now than ever. Lexi is the light of his life and he's as much in love with Iman as he was when they wed.

"They are not part of the New York party scene. Yes, they may go out to eat with friends such as Lou Reed, but he's happiest with his family."

Recent projects include designing a child's lunchbox and vocal stints on Lexi's favourite show, SpongeBob, as well as a part in the children's film, Arthur And The Invincibles, which also features Madonna and Snoop Dogg.

Bowie himself admits he is now "a lot more David Jones", adding: "I'm now probably truer to my real nature than I ever have been. And it's wonderful."

RIGHT With his Outstanding Achievement award at the GQ Men of the Year Awards at the Natural History Museum in London in 2002

Performing at the Glastonbury Festival in 2002. He first appeared there in 1971

RIGHT AND BELOW
Live in concert in 2003
as part of The Reality
Tour at Wembley
Arena in London

ABOVE David Bowie performs on stage at the relaunch of the Carling Apollo, Hammersmith, west London, in 2002

RIGHT Live at the Isle Of Wight Festival at Seaclose Park in 2004

LEFT In full cry as part of The Reality Tour at the Manchester Evening News Arena in Manchester

BELOW Another shot from his gig at the Hammersmith Apollo in 2002

I'M A LUCKY MAN

Bowie's philosophy on life, as revealed in his later years:

"I try to make every day matter. I've found that if you accumulate enough of those days, you feel fulfilled. You go to bed at night and say, 'I worked to the best of my abilities. I did my best to mend bridges. I didn't hurt anybody.'

"I am an extremely lucky and happy man. I have a wonderful relationship. I'm fulfilled in my work. I feel very comfortable with my existence right now."

" I HAVE A SERIES OF ENTHUSIASMS WHICH I HAVE IMMERSED MYSELF IN. EVER SINCE I WAS A KID I ALWAYS LOVED THE NEW THING

Ziggy played guitar
Jamming good with Weird and Gilly
And the Spiders from Mars
He played it left hand
But he made it too far
Became the Special Man
Then we were Ziggy's band

Ziggy really sang
Screwed up eyes and screw down hairdo
Like some cat from Japan
He could lick 'em by smiling
He could leave em to hang
Came on so loaded, man
Well hung and snow white tan

So where was the Spiders
while the Fly tried to break our balls
Just beer-light to guide us
So we bitched about his fans
and should we crush both his hands

Ziggy played for time
Jiving us that we was Voodoo
The Kids was just crass
He was the Nazz
With God-given Ass
He took it all too far
But boy could he play guitar

A series of exhibits
from the David Bowie
exhibition at the V&A
museum in London
that contained many
items from the life and
works of the musical
innovator and cultural
icon including the
original lyrics of the
song *Ziggy Stardust*

DAVID BOWIE:
A LIFE IN MOMENTS

1992

April – Appears at the Freddie Mercury Tribute Concert following the Queen frontman's death the year before. As well as performing *Heroes* and *All The Young Dudes*, he was joined on *Under Pressure* by Annie Lennox.

1990

October – A decade after his divorce from Angie, Bowie meets Somali-born supermodel Iman. He recalled: "I was naming the children the night we met... it was absolutely immediate."

1983

April 14 – Bowie reaches a new peak of popularity and commercial success in 1983 with the album *Let's Dance* which is co-produced by Chic's Nile Rodgers. The album goes platinum in both the UK and the US.

1977

September 11 – Bowie performs a duet with Bing Crosby of *Little Drummer Boy* and *Peace on Earth*. Crosby died a month later. On September 20, Bowie was pictured attending Mark Bolan's funeral after his tragic death.

1992

April 24 – Marries Iman Mohamed Abdulmajid at Lausanne register office in Switzerland. Guests include Bono, Yoko Ono and Eric Idle.

1997

January 9 – Bowie's 50th birthday concert features the Foo Fighters and the Smashing Pumpkins with the proceeds going to Save the Children.

2000

August 15 – Alexandria Zahra Jones, Bowie and Iman's daughter, is born.

2004

June 18 – Has a heart attack, one of six he had, after suffering chest pain while performing at the Hurricane Festival in Scheesel, Germany.

1947

January 8 – Born in Brixton, south London, Bowie was christened David Robert Jones.

1964

June 5 – First ever release – *Liza Jane/Louie Louie Go Home* – under the name of Davie Jones with The King-Bees. Only 3,500 copies were made.

1965

September 16 – Changes his name to David Bowie. He chose Bowie because it was: "the ultimate American knife. It is the medium for a conglomerate of statements and illusions".

1966

January 14 – First single released under his new name is *Can't Help Thinking About Me*. Bowie goes on to sell more than 135 million albums.

1975

March 7 – *Young Americans*, the ninth studio album, is released. While touring, Bowie creates the Thin White Duke persona but the massive amounts of cocaine he consumed during this period made his personality erratic and paranoid and he said that he lived on "red peppers, cocaine, and milk".

1972

June 16 – Bowie releases the iconic album *The Rise and Fall of Ziggy Stardust and the Spiders from Mars*, which tells the story of a bisexual alien rock superstar. The record goes to number 5 in the UK charts and today is regularly voted one of the greatest records ever.

1971

May 30 – After marrying in 1970, Angie gives birth to a son the pair name Zowie, though he later changes his name to Duncan. Duncan works as a film director and made the 2007 film 'Moon'.

1969

Spring – Meets Angie Barnett while living with his lover and landlady Mary Finnigan and her two children in South London. The three launch the Beckenham Arts Lab in South London and put on a weekly folk club.

2006

November – During a brief set at the Hammerstein Ballroom for Manhattan's annual Blackball charity concert, Bowie is joined by Alicia Keys for *Changes*. It is the last time Bowie performs his music on stage.

2013

A sell-out exhibition of Bowie artefacts, called "David Bowie Is", is shown at the V&A Museum featuring clothes, sleeve artwork and excerpts of film.

2014

February 19 – Bowie becomes the oldest recipient of a Brit Award in the ceremony's history when he wins the award for Best British Male, which is collected on his behalf by Kate Moss wearing his Ziggy Stardust costume. His acceptance speech makes reference to the Scottish independence referendum and his wish for the Scots to stay in the United Kingdom.

2016

January 8 – Bowie releases the studio album *Blackstar* to rave reviews – just two days before his death from liver cancer.

DISCOGRAPHY

The UK back catalogue of one of the most prolific artists in history

ALBUMS

DATE FIRST CHARTED	TITLE	LABEL	PEAK POSITION	WEEKS ON CHART	WEEKS @ NO.1
UNCHARTED	**DERAM**	DERAM	00	00	00
01.07.1972	**THE RISE AND FALL OF ZIGGY STARDUST AND THE SPIDERS FROM MARS**	RCA VICTOR	05	168	00
23.09.1972	**HUNKY DORY**	RCA VICTOR	03	132	00
25.11. 1972	**SPACE ODDITY**	RCA VICTOR	17	37	00
25.11. 1972	**THE MAN WHO SOLD THE WORLD**	RCA VICTOR	24	30	00
05.05.1973	**ALADDIN SANE**	RCA VICTOR	01	73	05
03.11. 1973	**PIN UPS**	RCA VICTOR	01	36	05
08.06.1974	**DIAMOND DOGS**	RCA VICTOR	01	35	04
16.11. 1974	**DAVID LIVE**	RCA VICTOR	02	13	00
05.04.1975	**YOUNG AMERICANS**	RCA VICTOR	02	12	00
07.02.1976	**STATION TO STATION**	RCA VICTOR	05	17	00
12.06.1976	**CHANGESONEBOWIE**	RCA VICTOR	02	28	00
29.01.1977	**LOW**	RCA VICTOR	02	23	00
29.10.1977	**HEROES**	RCA VICTOR	03	26	00
14.10.1978	**STAGE**	RCA VICTOR	05	10	00
09.06.1979	**LODGER**	RCA VICTOR	04	17	00
27.09.1980	**SCARY MONSTERS AND SUPER CREEPS**	RCA	01	32	02
10.01.1981	**VERY BEST OF DAVID BOWIE**	TEL	03	20	00
28.11.1981	**CHANGESTWOBOWIE**	RCA	24	17	00
15.01.1983	**RARE**	RCA	34	11	00
23.04.1983	**LET'S DANCE**	EMI AMERICA	01	56	03
20.08.1983	**GOLDEN YEARS**	RCA	33	05	00
05.11. 1983	**ZIGGY STARDUST – THE MOTION PICTURE**	EMI	17	07	00

28.04.1984	FAME AND FASHION (BOWIE'S ALL TIME GREATEST HITS)	RCA	40	06	00
19.05.1984	LOVE YOU TILL TUESDAY	DERAM	53	04	00
06.10.1984	TONIGHT	EMI AMERICA	01	19	01
05.07.1986	LABYRINTH (OST)	EMI AMERICA	38	02	00
02.05.1987	NEVER LET ME DOWN	EMI AMERICA	06	16	00
24.03.1990	CHANGESBOWIE	EMI	01	31	01
14.04.1990	HUNKY DORY (1990 VERSION)	EMI	39	02	00
14.04.1990	SPACE ODDITY (1990 VERSION)	EMI	64	01	00
14.04.1990	THE MAN WHO SOLD THE WORLD (1990 VERSION)	EMI	66	01	00
23.06.1990	THE RISE AND FALL OF ZIGGY STARDUST AND THE SPIDERS FROM MARS (1990 VERSION)	EMI	17	12	00
28.07.1990	ALADDIN SANE (1990 VERSION)	EMI	43	01	00
28.07.1990	PIN UPS (1990 VERSION)	EMI	52	01	00
27.10.1990	DIAMOND DOGS (1990 VERSION)	EMI	67	01	00
04.05.1991	YOUNG AMERICANS (1991 VERSION)	EMI	54	01	00
04.05.1991	STATION TO STATION (1991 VERSION)	EMI	57	01	00
07.09.1991	LOW (1990 VERSION)	EMI	64	01	00
17.04.1993	BLACK TIE WHITE NOISE	ARISTA	01	11	01
20.11.1993	THE SINGLES COLLECTION	EMI	09	35	00
07.05.1994	SANTA MONICA '72	GOLDEN YEARS	74	01	00
07.10.1995	OUTSIDE	RCA	08	06	00
15.02.1997	EARTHLING	RCA	06	04	00
08.11.1997	THE BEST OF 1969/1974	EMI	13	27	00
02.05.1998	THE BEST OF 1974/1979	EMI	39	03	00
16.10.1999	HOURS...	VIRGIN	05	06	00
07.10.2000	BOWIE AT THE BEEB	EMI	07	05	00
22.06.2002	HEATHEN	COLUMBIA	05	20	00
20.07.2002	THE RISE AND FALL OF ZIGGY STARDUST	EMI	36	03	00
16.11. 2002	BEST OF BOWIE	EMI	11	119	00
27.09.2003	REALITY	COLUMBIA	03	05	00
19.11. 2005	THE PLATINUM COLLECTION	EMI	53	05	00
31.03.2007	THE BEST OF - 1980/1987	EMI	34	02	00
12.07.2008	LIVE SANTA MONICA '72	EMI	61	01	00
06.02.2010	A REALITY TOUR	SONY MUSIC	53	01	00

23.03.2013	THE NEXT DAY	RCA	01	29	01
16.11.2013	THE NEXT DAY EXTRA	RCA	89	01	00
04.10.2014	SOUND & VISION	RHINO	63	01	00
29.11.2014	NOTHING HAS CHANGED - THE VERY BEST OF	RCA/RHINO	09	32	00
08.10.2015	FIVE YEARS - 1969-1973	PARLOPHONE	45	01	00
08.01.2016	BLACKSTAR	RCA	-	-	-

SINGLES

DATE FIRST CHARTED	TITLE	LABEL	PEAK POSITION	WEEKS ON CHART	WEEKS @ NO.1
06.09.1969	SPACE ODDITY	PHILIPS	05	14	00
24.06.1972	STARMAN	RCA	10	11	00
16.09.1972	JOHN I'M ONLY DANCING	RCA	12	10	00
09.12.1972	THE JEAN GENIE	RCA	02	13	00
14.04.1973	DRIVE-IN SATURDAY	RCA	03	10	00
30.06.1973	LIFE ON MARS	RCA	03	16	00
15.09.1973	LAUGHING GNOME	DERAM	06	12	00
20.10.1973	SORROW	RCA	03	15	00
23.02.1974	REBEL REBEL	RCA	05	07	00
20.04.1974	ROCK AND ROLL SUICIDE	RCA	22	07	00
22.06.1974	DIAMOND DOGS	RCA	21	06	00
28.09.1974	KNOCK ON WOOD	RCA	10	06	00
01.03.1975	YOUNG AMERICANS	RCA	18	07	00
02.08.1975	FAME	RCA	17	08	00
11.10.1975	SPACE ODDITY {1975}	RCA	01	10	02
29.11.1975	GOLDEN YEARS	RCA	08	10	00
22.05.1976	TVC15	RCA	33	04	00
19.02.1977	SOUND AND VISION	RCA	03	11	00
15.10.1977	HEROES	RCA	24	08	00
21.01.1978	BEAUTY AND THE BEAST	RCA	39	03	00
02.12.1978	BREAKING GLASS (EP)	RCA	54	07	00
05.05.1979	BOYS KEEP SWINGING	RCA	07	10	00
21.07. 1979	DJ	RCA	29	05	00
15.12.1979	JOHN I'M ONLY DANCING (AGAIN)	RCA	12	08	00
01.03.1980	ALABAMA SONG	RCA	23	05	00
16.08.1980	ASHES TO ASHES	RCA	01	10	02
01.11.1980	FASHION	RCA	05	12	00
10.01.1981	SCARY MONSTERS (AND SUPER CREEPS)	RCA	20	06	00
28.03.1981	UP THE HILL BACKWARDS	RCA	32	06	00
14.11.1981	UNDER PRESSURE with Queen	EMI	01	11	02
28.11.1981	WILD IS THE WIND	RCA	24	10	00
06.03.1982	BAAL'S HYMN (EP)	RCA	29	05	00
10.04.1982	CAT PEOPLE (PUTTING OUT FIRE)	MCA	26	06	00
27.11.1982	PEACE ON EARTH/LITTLE DRUMMER BOY with Bing Crosby	RCA	03	10	00
26.03.1983	LET'S DANCE	EMI AMERICA	01	16	03

Date	Title	Label			
11.06.1983	CHINA GIRL	EMI AMERICA	02	08	00
18.06.1983	SPACE ODDITY (1983)	NO-LABEL	85	03	00
18.06.1983	THE JEAN GENIE (1983)	NO-LABEL	98	02	00
25.06.1983	LIFE ON MARS (1983)	NO-LABEL	97	01	00
24.09.1983	MODERN LOVE	EMI AMERICA	02	08	00
05.11.1983	WHITE LIGHT/WHITE HEAT	RCA	46	03	00
22.09.1984	BLUE JEAN	EMI AMERICA	06	09	00
08.12.1984	TONIGHT	EMI AMERICA	53	05	00
09.02.1985	THIS IS NOT AMERICA with The Pat Metheny Group	EMI AMERICA	14	08	00
08.06.1985	LOVING THE ALIEN	EMI AMERICA	19	09	00
07.09.1985	DANCING IN THE STREET with Mick Jagger	EMI AMERICA	01	15	04
15.03.1986	ABSOLUTE BEGINNERS	VIRGIN	02	09	00
21.06.1986	UNDERGROUND	EMI AMERICA	21	07	00
08.11.1986	WHEN THE WIND BLOWS	VIRGIN	44	04	00
04.04.1987	DAY-IN DAY-OUT	EMI AMERICA	17	06	00
27.06.1987	TIME WILL CRAWL	EMI AMERICA	33	04	00
29.08.1987	NEVER LET ME DOWN	EMI AMERICA	34	06	00
07.04.1990	FAME 90 (GASS MIX)	EMI-USA	28	04	00
22.08.1992	REAL COOL WORLD	WARNER BROTHERS	53	01	00
27.03.1993	JUMP THEY SAY	ARISTA	09	06	00
12.06.1993	BLACK TIE WHITE NOISE Featuring T AL B SURE	ARISTA	36	02	00
23.10.1993	MIRACLE GOODNIGHT	ARISTA	40	02	00
04.12.1993	THE BUDDHA OF SUBURBIA	ARISTA	35	03	00
23.09.1995	THE HEARTS FILTHY LESSON	RCA	35	02	00
02.12.1995	STRANGERS WHEN WE MEET/THE MAN WHO...	RCA	39	02	00
02.03.1996	HALLO SPACEBOY	RCA	12	04	00
16.11.1996	TELLING LIES	RCA	76	01	00
08.02.1997	LITTLE WONDER	RCA	14	03	00
26.04.1997	DEAD MAN WALKING	RCA	32	02	00
30.08.1997	SEVEN YEARS IN TIBET	RCA	61	02	00
21.02.1998	I CAN'T READ	VELVEL	73	02	00
02.10.1999	THURSDAY'S CHILD	VIRGIN	16	05	00
18.12.1999	UNDER PRESSURE with Queen	PARLOPHONE	14	09	00
05.02.2000	SURVIVE	VIRGIN	28	02	00
29.07.2000	SEVEN	VIRGIN	32	02	00
11.05.2002	LOVING THE ALIEN Scumfrog vs Bowie	POSITIVA	41	02	00
29.06.2002	SLOW BURN	COLUMBIA	94	01	00
28.09.2002	EVERYONE SAYS HI	COLUMBIA	20	03	00
12.07.2003	JUST FOR ONE DAY (HEROES) David Guetta vs Bowie	Virgin	73	02	00
26.06.2004	REBEL NEVER GETS OLD	COLUMBIA	47	02	00
22.12.2007	PEACE ON EARTH/LITTLE DRUMMER BOY with Bing Crosby	CAPITOL	73	02	00
19.01.2013	WHERE ARE WE NOW	COLUMBIA	06	02	00
29.11.2014	SUE (OR IN A SEASON OF CRIME)	RHINO	81	01	00

Discography taken from officialcharts.com

Some albums charted some time later than they were released

ST★R
IN THE
SKY

From Brixton to Brooklyn,
when the news broke,
mourners showed their
love and admiration
with floral shrines and
a mass sing-along...

A WORLD IN
MOURNING
Tributes pour in
for Bowie as the
media react to
the shock news

David Bowie's entire career was based on surprise and shock. Unfortunately, this included his death as well.

When news broke on January 11 that Bowie had passed away after an 18-month battle with liver cancer, there was disbelief across the globe. In an age of instant media, of Twitter and Facebook and Instagram, the fact Bowie had managed to keep his plight under wraps for so long only heightened the profound sense of loss.

His legion of fans had no time to prepare, no time to ready themselves for the day his passing would be announced. It was classic Bowie. A final twist in a life that was forever a performance. And perhaps the signs were there...

Bowie released his latest album on his 69th birthday and *Blackstar* included a track called *Lazarus* that contained the words: *"Look up here, I'm in heaven,"* a profoundly prophetic line from a man who knew he did not have much time left.

Tony Visconti, one of the producers of *Blackstar* and a long-time collaborator with Bowie confirmed that his passing was one final act in a lifetime full of wonderful performances.

"He always did what he wanted to do," Visconti said. "And he wanted to do it his way and he wanted to do it the best way. His death was no different from his life – a work of art."

Death and dying are often surrounded by black humour and Bowie's was no different. It has emerged that the final Twitter account Bowie followed before he passed away was God's account – @theTweetofGod – a dark and humorous touch by a showman to the end.

Although Bowie's family and close friends will have had some time to come to terms with his expected passing, the rest of the world had to wake up to the cruel news and the response was epic.

Aside from the reactions of fellow musicians, dignitaries and celebrities across the world, Bowie's death was also mourned and remembered by all those who were touched by his musical genius.

In his home town of Brixton, hundreds – if not thousands – gathered at an impromptu shrine outside Morleys department store which has a huge painting of Bowie on the side. Stood seven or eight deep, fans sang his music, chatted, cried and swapped Bowie stories.

Across town, Heddon Street – which featured

> ## JANUARY 10 2016 – DAVID BOWIE DIED PEACEFULLY TODAY SURROUNDED BY HIS FAMILY AFTER A COURAGEOUS 18-MONTH BATTLE WITH CANCER

– THE OFFICIAL STATEMENT ANNOUNCING BOWIE'S DEATH

on the cover of *The Rise and Fall of Ziggy Stardust and the Spiders From Mars* – was also inundated with fans, floral wreaths and tears. Across the Atlantic, Bowie's star on the Hollywood Walk of Fame was covered in flowers, as was the doorstep of Bowie's New York address.

Although it may feel to many that his death is too early, the reaction across the globe should bring comfort to those who knew Bowie best. Nobody knows what legacy he wanted to leave nor what he wanted the world to think of him when he was gone. However, as tributes and memories go, packed streets full of people having a wonderful time, coming together to sing his music, share kind words, dance and laugh takes some beating.

He would have loved it.

TOP A makeshift memorial surrounds Bowie's star on the Hollywood Walk of Fame in Los Angeles

LEFT Tributes arrive outside his former home in Brixton and at his apartment in New York

LEFT AND BELOW
Mourners leave flowers and
messages of condolence as
they remember a legend
and his iconic individuality

ABOVE Crowds gather at the mural of
Bowie in Brixton as tears give way to cheers
during a mass dance and sing-along

" HE ALWAYS DID WHAT HE WANTED TO DO. AND HE WANTED TO DO IT HIS WAY AND HE WANTED TO DO IT THE BEST WAY. HIS DEATH WAS NO DIFFERENT FROM HIS LIFE – A WORK OF ART "

- BOWIE'S LIFE-LONG COLLABORATOR, PRODUCER TONY VISCONTI

" David's friendship was the light of my life. I never met such a brilliant person. " He was the best there is

- IGGY POP

" I'M DEVASTATED. DAVID BOWIE CHANGED THE COURSE OF MY LIFE FOREVER. I FOUND HIM SO INSPIRING AND INNOVATIVE. UNIQUE AND PROVOCATIVE. A REAL GENIUS. HIS MUSIC WAS ALWAYS INSPIRING BUT SEEING HIM LIVE SET ME OFF ON A JOURNEY THAT, FOR ME, I HOPE WILL NEVER END. THANK YOU DAVID BOWIE. I OWE YOU A LOT. THE WORLD WILL MISS YOU "

- MADONNA

" We all look towards what he did. We're all still walking in his slipstream. We're all still many, many yards behind what he was doing. Because he led the way. He was the leader, he was the governor "

- ULTRAVOX'S MIDGE URE

" David's death came as a complete surprise, as did nearly everything else about him. I feel a huge gap now. I received an email from him seven days ago. It was as funny as always, and as surreal, looping through word games and allusions and all the usual stuff we did. It ended with this sentence: 'Thank you for our good times, Brian. They will never rot'. And it was signed 'Dawn'. I realise now he was saying goodbye "

- BRIAN ENO

" Very sad news to wake up to on this raining morning. David was a great star and I treasure the moments we had together. His music played a very strong part in British musical history and I'm proud to think of the huge influence he has had on people all around the world. I send my deepest sympathies to his family and will always remember the great laughs we had through the years. His star will shine in the sky forever "

- SIR PAUL MCCARTNEY

" WE HAD SO MANY GOOD TIMES TOGETHER. HE WAS MY FRIEND. I WILL NEVER FORGET HIM "

- THE ROLLING STONES' MICK JAGGER

" SO, WE MOURN THE LOSS OF A GREAT TALENT. WE THINK ABOUT HIS FAMILY AND FRIENDS, WHO HAVE LOST A LOVED ONE TOO EARLY, BUT I THINK ALSO WE CELEBRATE AN IMMENSE BRITISH TALENT WHO HAS ENRICHED ALL OF OUR LIVES "

- PRIME MINISTER DAVID CAMERON

" As soon as I heard of his death, very, very sad, *Life On Mars* comes flowing back into my mind. Wonderful song, wonderful guy "

- LABOUR LEADER JEREMY CORBYN

" Over here on E Street, we're feeling the great loss of David Bowie. Always changing and ahead of the curve, he was an artist whose excellence you aspired to "

- BRUCE SPRINGSTEEN

" For those who were his fans, he was a charismatic and exotic creature and still gloriously beautiful even as he approached 70. But face to face he was funny, clever, well-read, excited by the arts, and really good company. We have also lost a wonderful clown whose combined sense of mischief and creativity delightedly touched our hearts. David Bowie was my Salvador Dali "

- THE WHO'S PETE TOWNSHEND

" DAVID BOWIE WAS ONE OF MY MOST IMPORTANT INSPIRATIONS, SO FEARLESS, SO CREATIVE, HE GAVE US MAGIC FOR A LIFETIME "

- KANYE WEST

" I JUST LOST A HERO. RIP DAVID BOWIE "

- RICKY GERVAIS

'FOR ME, LIFE IS ABOUT THE MOMENT. YOU CAN'T LIVE WITH RIDICULOUS EXPECTATIONS OF THE FUTURE'

David Bowie, 1947-2016